Martin Hawes is the best-selling author of twenty books on personal finance as well as a regular contributor to financial columns in the media. He is widely regarded for his ability to explain complex financial issues in ways that people can understand and apply.

Martin was a successful business consultant for more than ten years and now provides individualised wealth planning to help clients become wealthy and free to pursue their dreams.

Martin Hawes is sixty years old and lives in Queenstown, New Zealand. His interests include rock climbing, mountaineering (in 1995 he attempted Mt Everest), skiing, and cycling.

Martin is an Authorised Financial Adviser and his Disclosure Statement is available free of charge at www.martinhawes.com.

TWENTY GOOD
SUMMERS

Work less, live more and make the most of your money

MARTIN HAWES

FULLY UPDATED AND REVISED EDITION

ALLEN&UNWIN
SYDNEY · MELBOURNE · AUCKLAND · LONDON

First published by Allen & Unwin in 2006
This revised edition published in 2012

Copyright © Martin Hawes 2012

Allen & Unwin
Sydney, Melbourne, Auckland, London

83 Alexander Street
Crows Nest NSW 2065
Australia
Phone: (61 2) 8425 0100
Fax: (61 2) 9906 2218
Email: info@allenandunwin.com
Web: www.allenandunwin.com

Cataloguing-in-Publication details are available
from the National Library of Australia
www.trove.nla.gov.au

ISBN 978 1 74237 806 0

Set in 12/15 pt Adobe Garamond Pro by Bookhouse, Sydney
Printed in Australia by McPherson's Printing Group

10 9 8 7 6 5 4 3 2 1

This book is dedicated to the memory of Paul Scaife, who died on Mt Tasman on New Year's Eve 2003.

Contents

Section 3 **Making it work**

Foreword

Since the first edition of this book was published, I have learned a great deal. From all the presentations that I have done and clients I have worked with, I have learned much about the way that people plan for and face retirement. There is no doubt that people find the whole idea of stopping full-time work and giving up a steady monthly pay check as scary—it creates insecurity at the very time when life should seem secure. It's a major development stage to be traversed at the very time when we are not terribly good at change, and it is not just financial change. There is plenty of change happening at this time beyond the need to make ends meet from investment returns—there is change within the family, change to your social status, change to how you spend your days and change to your health, to name a few.

However, over and over again I find that it is the change of investment strategy that causes the most anxiety. The prospect of a changing financial situation is difficult—from growing wealth, usually with a regular salary, to being dependent on the performance of financial markets for your income is a major shift.

Many people receive a lump sum from the sale of a business or cashing in superannuation funds as they start to ease back into some kind of retirement but, of course, few of us get much practice before then at investing lump sums. When the lump sum is received, we know that this is it—we need to look after it because this is all we are going to get. The pressure is great and some people do not invest their money well —they either default into bank deposits, which are generally safe but give a low return, or go into other inappropriate, generally higher-risk investments that lose money. If there is one thing that the Global Financial Crisis should have taught us, it is that bad stuff does happen and a careful, well-thought-out diversified investment strategy is essential. In any event, it is most likely that the investment strategy that got you to retirement will not serve you in retirement.

People go into their twenty good summers financially fearful—and so they should. Provided that this fear does not encourage them into an excessively low-risk investment plan, a bit of anxiety is a good thing. After all, you have the whole of the rest of your life on the line.

For several years now, cash yield has been difficult to achieve—property yields are low, bond yields abysmal and share dividends fairly ordinary. A lack of cash yield leads some who are reliant on their investment capital for income into strange investment decisions. Much of the packaging of sub-prime mortgages into bonds and the like was driven by the quest for yield, just like the boom and bust of finance companies and Icelandic banks.

I have long thought that retired investors should adopt a fairly conventional investment strategy that includes investments, like shares, that pay low dividends knowing that they can periodically skim off some of their capital profits by selling a few units when the market is up.

Investing for capital growth like this is fairly safe, provided that you do not become a forced seller. Forced sellers nearly always have to sell when the market is down because they need cash, which is obviously a disaster. Chapter 20 has been added to this edition to show how holding some cash can act as a buffer to get you through the tough times when the market is down—you will still be able to carry on buying the groceries without having to sell out.

When I came to revisit this book, I had thought that I might push the reset button. Now, as a sixty year old, it is tempting to say that sixty is the new fifty and so I could start to count my twenty good summers from about now. However, when I think about it, I do not want to do that. The whole idea of Twenty Good Summers is that the time ahead of me is getting shorter and this is a positive motivator to get on and do the things that I have always wanted to do.

In fact, a few people have (fairly gently) taken me to task about the idea of Twenty Good Summers. These people tell me that I am counting my life down, that it is a very negative thing to think about and that I may fall victim to some kind of self-fulfilling prophecy. In other words, if I think that I have twenty summers left, that is the number I will get, instead of, possibly, a much greater number. These comments miss my point.

First, I have always made it clear that I would like to have twenty summers for fairly extreme things like alpine climbing and ski mountaineering. That doesn't mean I think that my life will be over after that, even though Joan tells me if I wear my crampons inside one more time I definitely will be history—well within twenty summers. In fact, I am trying to program myself to live to a ripe old age. It's just that I probably won't be doing some of the things at seventy that I am doing now.

The second reason I do not think the idea is negative at all is that I use it as a motivator. I have stopped saying that I will do something 'one day' and, instead, ask myself 'why not today?' The basic idea of this book is compelling—it is time to get on with it!

The third reason I do not think the idea is negative is that it seems to me that thinking of a series of good summers is better than 'retirement'. I still think that word, retirement, has negative connotations and one thing that I have *not* learned since the first edition of this book is a better word for it. To me, retirement still implies withdrawing and living an inactive life. Even though I know that many 'retired' people live very full and fulfilling lives, I don't like the word.

Although some people have not warmed to the central idea and phrase of the book, many others have and they will often tell me how the book has changed their lives for the better. I have given many talks on this title and I know that people have made big changes in their lives after reading the book. Some have sold businesses and others have given up full-time work to get on with the things that they have always wanted to do.

So, the first book, as it was originally written, is still here, but with a good number of additions. I have inserted two new chapters and numerous breakout boxes providing new material learned from my clients over the years.

We have also had another economic meltdown since the first edition and I have seen close up, once again, the effect that such things have on people depending on investment capital for their income. At the point of retirement, people are at a crossroads and they will usually take a different path from the one they have been following for several decades. This intersection needs to be approached with care—the booms and busts of the economic cycle can wreck lives and you do not want yours to be part of the rubble.

Older people need to act conservatively and cautiously. They are no longer in a position to greatly enhance their financial position. In fact, they can only really mess it up. This is a time for good advice. I know that sometimes it is hard to find—financial advisers are often implicated in financial crashes, as I have seen over the last thirty years. Nevertheless, not all professionals are ratbags and if you think that dealing with a good professional is expensive, just wait until you have taken advice from an amateur.

We will all necessarily worry about whether or not we have enough money. Although this book tackles that question head on, calculating how much you need is very difficult. This is made more difficult by advances in healthcare as medical science continues to make major progression; for example, things like stem-cell therapies and other biotech breakthroughs mean potential medical treatments for a whole range of complaints become possible.

This has financial ramifications: we should live longer, although this will require money. Many of the new treatments that are becoming available are expensive and may not be available unless you pay. Health has always been a financial issue—those with money live longer and this is about to become even more obvious than it was, as all sorts of treatments become available to keep our battered old bodies going, and give us really good quality of life for longer. If you are planning to spend your capital in retirement you will need more of it: first to keep you alive, and second because you will be spending for longer.

Arriving at the crossroads of retirement is a time for big decisions and we all have to ask ourselves some big questions: What do we want? How do we want to live for the rest of our lives? What is truly important? Then we need to go out and get it or make it happen. A new life has to be resourced—we need money, as always—but this book offers a fairly optimistic view of the amount that is needed. Provided you are prepared to make some compromises, such as working a bit longer or carrying on part time, or downsizing the house, you may be able to have the life that you want right now. In any event, retiring or continuing to work part time or full time, you will never be better—fitter and more capable of doing things—than you are right now. The original message still stands: it is time to get on with it and enjoy some good summers.

Martin Hawes
October 2012

Section | 1

PLANNING

1 | Twenty good summers

Ten years ago, I turned fifty. Any birthday which has a zero on the end is always a bit of a wake-up call, but for some reason my fiftieth in particular was accompanied by feelings that time was sliding by. I have always been heavily involved in the outdoors—mountaineering, climbing, hiking and skiing—and I was starting to feel that there were more things to do than I was ever going to have time available to do them. I kept looking at mountains to climb and trips to go on and thinking, 'How am I ever going to have time to do all this stuff before I get properly old?' On my fiftieth birthday, I spent the day climbing frozen waterfalls. From the top, I could see the vastness that is the Southern Alps of New Zealand and said (for the hundredth time) to my climbing mate, 'So little time—so much to do!'

This got me thinking: maybe I only have twenty good summers left—just twenty good summers to enjoy the mountains and do the other things that I love. In twenty summers I would be seventy (my allotted three score and ten). Hopefully, at that age I won't be dead and I will still be enjoying life—I know lots of people in their seventies, eighties and even in their nineties who are still very active and enjoying life. But chances are that by the time I am seventy, I won't be doing a lot of the things that I love at the moment—I probably won't be out climbing, doing seminars, biking, skiing and so forth. I may have only twenty good summers to do these kinds of things. Perhaps I won't get even that number, and I am surely not going to get a whole lot more than twenty even if luck is on my side.

Well, last year my twenty good summers came down to twelve good summers; and by the time you're reading this book it will be down to ten . . . Time no longer stretches forever in front of me, with endless potential. These are small, finite numbers—never-never land is starting to look like it doesn't exist! It really is time to act, to live the life that I want. Assuming that this life on Earth is the only life we have, and evidence to the contrary is not particularly great, now is the time to live it to the full—to spend the remaining summers wisely, making each one count. Now is the time to be as free as possible to do the things that I have always wanted to do. Maybe I will get more than twenty good summers to go climbing, but I am not prepared to bet on it!

I have told this story at seminars many times now. It always strikes a chord, especially with people of a similar age to me—that is, the generation known as Baby Boomers. They recognise that, in spite of what they thought in the past, they are not going to be forever young, and that if there was ever a time to take dramatic steps to live the life that they want, that time is now.

I am a quintessential Baby Boomer. By and large, we Baby Boomers have had a very comfortable, easy existence. We are used to having it every which way, with the lifestyle we wanted and a high level of comfort. We don't want to work now, or at least not so hard, but we don't want to go without. As a generation we've had it very good, with no world wars, no depressions, no epidemics, nothing to spoil our easy existence. And we want to keep things good!

Some of us are still wondering what we are going to do when we grow up. We invented sex. We are starting to discover middle age and tell each other that it does not really start at forty but at fifty, and we will push that out to sixty when we need to. No doubt sometime soon we will invent death and dying! At least it will seem like it. Having established the permissive society, now we want to give ourselves permission to work less and live more. These are the things that characterise the Baby Boomers—the 'now' generation.

Most importantly, there are lots of us and we have always been able to dominate simply because of our numbers. As we come to our numerical peak and take political control and, therefore, control of our nations' cheque books, we will continue our dominance. That there are so many of us makes a big difference to what happens across society, including the economy and business markets. That there are so many of us is important to business, as we create trends that businesses can sell to. It is also important in that while there are a lot of us—before we start to die off, which is likely to start happening very soon—governments will have to support us as we age.

This sizeable generation of people who thought they would never grow old *is* starting to want to change what they do. We have always said that we would never retire—retirement is a swear word to many Baby Boomers, who think it means giving up and withdrawing from society. So, ever inventive, we have tried to come up with a new word for it. 'Lifestyle'—more and more, we want to surrender our jobs and our houses in the suburbs to pursue a new lifestyle. Look at the evidence—we are flocking to the coast or to small farms on the edges of cities. People are downsizing their houses and their jobs to live near a beach or in the country, or are moving into lock-and-leave apartments in order to be able to work less and play more. The result: higher prices for coastal land and floods of people buying holiday homes or apartments in the mountains or on a beach.

Truth be told, Baby Boomers are probably starting to get tired. Some of us have had high-pressure jobs requiring us to work hard for years, and now the generation that believed it would never age and never want to retire is starting to feel the need to slow down. We do not want to admit that we are starting to age and really *want* to 'slow down' so we are seeking this thing called lifestyle but, really, lifestyle is a euphemism for retirement that saves us from having to use the dreaded 'R' word. Because there are so many of us this is making a huge difference to property and other markets, and will continue to make a difference for twenty years or so yet.

Retirement

I only use the word 'retirement' because no one has come up with a better substitute that is not long-winded, and because everyone knows what it means. I do not like the word because it is a derivative of the French word meaning to withdraw, and it has connotations of living a poor, mean and miserable life, hunched over a one-bar heater existing on re-used tea bags and plain biscuits. While that's a bit of an exaggeration I am sure that you know what I mean!

Yet, retirement is a fairly new concept—most people in previous generations have had to work until they drop. It was really only in the late nineteenth century that the idea of a pension started to gain some currency and with it came the prospect of a few well-earned golden years following work (and, of course, most people in those days certainly wanted to escape work because it was generally hard, physical labour).

'Retirement' is changing: it now takes many forms and is not so much an event that might happen on one day, but is instead a process of winding down and easing back into another lifestyle. It often includes some work, travel, sports activities, travel and, as life expectancy continues to improve, will go on for some decades. It is quite a different idea from what it was—but I do not have a nice one-word description.

What does this lifestyle look like? Well, it means working less, having more time to do the things you haven't had time for in the past, enjoying living in a nice house in a nice place surrounded by good friends and family. It is not about buying a rocking chair, sitting in it and waiting twenty years to die. It is about being active in our hobbies, our gardens, our communities, on the beach or in the country, and active in our travel in the backblocks of home or to other countries. It may also mean being active in paid work—albeit not as active as before.

These are the things my clients have told me when they dream their dreams. For the last few years, I have been actively involved in WealthPlanning, helping people generate and arrange the money they need for the life they want. As part of each session with a new client, I ask about their ideas of a dream life. These are the things that nearly always come out: more time, more relaxation, travel, contribution to the community, time with the family and stepping back to enjoy the good things in life some more. Above all, the consistent theme is that people want to get out of the daily grind—to have more time, and the money and energy to enjoy it.

However, in easing back so that we can live the lives we want, we first need to sort our money out. Our parents might have called this retirement while we call it seeking 'lifestyle', but the problem is just the same—how do you fund the life you want when you are no longer part of the daily grind? How do we use the capital we *have* to obtain the passive income we *need* to be free? That is what this book is about.

This is a book for everyone who expects to work less and live off savings. Whether you are already at that point or aspire to be there in ten years' time, you need to know how to use your investment capital to supplement the money you will have from superannuation and, perhaps, from working.

This expectation poses some questions:

- How much money do we need to be free?
- How do we arrange that money to generate income?
- How can we continue to work, albeit not so hard or continuously?
- How do we access the capital in our biggest asset—the family home?

- How can we organise that money to maximise our income?

This book tries to answer these questions and show you how to use your money to give you the life that you want. However, it first assumes a couple of things:

- The first assumption is that you do have some capital—nothing comes from nothing and you cannot have financial freedom if you have to keep working as you are now. If you aspire to financial freedom you will have to set yourself a target for your wealth so that you can live the life of your dreams. I call it your 'Freedom Figure' and this is discussed in Section 2.
- The second assumption is that you want to work less and to enjoy a more peaceful and unhurried life—this is not to say that you will necessarily stop work altogether.

Lots of people happily work and run businesses well into their seventies and eighties. Stopping work completely is not the lifestyle of a lot of people's dreams. Even if you are financially able to live entirely off passive income, you may not want to—there is a lot of joy and a lot of pleasure for some of us in our work.

This is not a book on how to develop the wealth that you need to live the life you want—there are other books on that sort of thing. However, having said that, I hope it will serve as an inspiration to you to develop the wealth required to live the life of your dreams. If you do not yet have adequate money to be free, you need to set yourself a target or a goal so that you can continue to work and strive with an endgame in mind. That endgame is financial freedom—a position where your money and your time are your own.

Money is not an end in itself—it is the means that will allow you to live the lifestyle you want. My experience is that there are many people who have quite a lot of money but who do not have it properly arranged and invested in a way that will allow them to be free. Sometimes people do not know how or when to stop, how to say that they have enough—that now is the time to get on and do the things they have always wanted to do. The habit of a lifetime, the habit of building up wealth, can be hard to break. But the number of good summers is steadily diminishing. What follows is how to use your money to make the most of them.

2 | Making the break

It is hard to make changes. Breaking the habits of a lifetime is never going to be easy. You may have a very clear vision of the kind of life that you want, knowing what changes you want to make and understanding all too well the things you do not like about the way you currently live. You may have a strong feeling that time is slipping away, that now is the time for you to stop saying, 'One day I really want to . . .', and just go and do it. Nevertheless, despite all these things pushing you to a new life, it is hard to make the break.

Deciding to work less and live more is a great step into the unknown. For years you have been pushing in one direction along a road that many have travelled before. You have married, maybe had children, perhaps divorced, progressed your career with good promotions, perhaps developed a business, the children have left home . . .

Now, you have picked up a book about slowing down, working less, rearranging your finances and living a different life. You have picked the book up, and you are reading it! This is a journey into new territory—territory not so well travelled. And that is frightening. There is no one to tell you what the terrain in this new place is like, what and where the traps and pitfalls are, what to avoid and what to seek out. Given all this, it is not easy to move away from the security you have always known.

Well, some people have gone before you, and they have reported that this is not a territory full of snakes, crocodiles and other wild animals. In fact, the terrain is fairly soft and the weather benign—it is actually a pretty nice place. Certainly it is not heaven on Earth, full of milk and honey—there are things that can go wrong and traps for the unwary. But working less and living more is not a fearful way to live.

So what is stopping you? Experience through my WealthPlanning work has shown me a range of things that typically stop people. People do have their 'buts'. 'I would like to slow down, but . . .' It is very common for the 'but' they give to be an excuse, rather than the real reason for not making the break. Without digging too deeply into psychology and therefore moving into an area beyond my competence, I sometimes have to work quite hard to find people's real objection to taking action.

Here are some of the common things that I find stop people:

- Many people, even some who are quite wealthy, worry that their money will run out before they do. This is the most obvious and common fear, and it is dealt with in Chapter 8, Do we have enough? Suffice to say here that you may not need as much as you think. There is also the 'enough is never enough' syndrome, which is dealt with in Chapter 6.

  Depending on factors like how much you are going to continue to work, the investment returns you can obtain, and the lifestyle you want, you may well find you already have enough to live the life that you want.

- Stopping work makes people seem old. If you think of retiring as slowing down and working less as, you may fear that you will move into a space labelled 'Old Age'. That is not a great picture to place yourself in, and it is probably not accurate. Just because you have decided to travel more or to work from home that is not a reason to see yourself as suddenly being old.

- Many people are concerned about what family and friends will think. Will they think that you have lost it? That you are no longer up for the game? That you can no longer foot it in the real world? Some people will not care what others think about their change, others will feel they have to carefully craft a story to explain what they are doing.

- Some people have no clear picture of what they are moving towards. Most people know what they do not want; for example, a client who is a motor mechanic told me he did not want to have his head under a car bonnet any more. However, not only do you need to know what you do not want, you also need to know what you do want and have a clear picture of what your new life will be like.

- Some people's sense of self-worth is tied up in what they do. Both their status and feelings of belonging are tied firmly to their work. If, for example, they have been CEO of a large firm, they do not want to become 'just a consultant'.

- Many people fear being bored and/or lonely. There are people for whom work is nearly their whole life—they have friends from work, their work is their vocation and avocation and there is not much else in their lives.

- Personal relationships may get in the way. Spouses and partners may want to do different things with their time, or perhaps one does not want change while the other does. At times partners may make assumptions about what the other is thinking and feeling that are inaccurate; for example, someone may think their partner will never want to leave a much-loved and well-kept house and garden, while in reality the focus on house and garden has developed simply because there is nothing else to do in Cricklewood.

These are some of the things that stop people reaching out for the life that they say they want. Some of these things—in fact, most of them—are easily and obviously addressed and fixed. A bit of 'pull yourself together' talk is often all that is needed, although that is not always successful in breaking the shackles of insecurity. Many of the fears that people have are imaginary, being really the fear of the unknown—a sort of grown-up's version of being afraid of the dark. However, having said that, there are some things that you should be wary of, if not actually fearful of. Some pitfalls that you should watch for are:

- The money really could run out. Being too optimistic in terms of investment returns, having too rich a lifestyle, working less than you expected, or experiencing an unexpected setback like illness or even your partner's death, could make this fear a reality. You do need to approach this change to your life by planning with real assumptions and erring on the conservative side.
- You should know as much as you can about what you are jumping into. This is not a holiday for a few weeks—it is a change of lifestyle that is likely to be permanent. There is an old property-investment rule that you should not buy investment property when you are on holiday. For example, if you go to the Gold Coast for a couple of weeks, it is very

easy to get sucked into buying investment property on the basis of feelings of wellbeing generated by being on holiday. Planning to work less and live more is the same—it needs to be planned for with a good dose of reality on the side.

- Do not move to a place where you will not be able to do what you plan to. This particularly applies to work things—if you are a marketing expert and hope to get a couple of days' consulting work a week, moving to Cricklewood—where the only business is a general store—is not likely to provide much marketing consultancy work. This is not a problem if you have good contacts back in the city that will happily use your services, but it will be a disaster if you do not have the contacts you need before you make the move.

- Be very clear about how you are planning to spend your time. Some people who have decreased their workload say that they seem to be rushing around just as much as before, but not achieving what they want. You do need to continue to strive—life is hardly worthwhile if you just vegetate. Set goals, whether they are to get your rock-climbing grades up, your golf handicap down, books read and things learned, hours of work decreased, etc. Again, this is not a holiday for a few weeks—it is your new lifestyle and it's likely to continue to need a good bit of structuring and forward planning.

- Do not get too busy and successful in your work. If you have become self-employed, which is quite common for people wanting a better lifestyle, you may find that you actually get too busy. This is because you forget how to say 'no'. It has happened to me—embarrassingly, more than once—when I have simply taken on more than I should have. The word 'no' is very simple and you can permit yourself to use it.

Retirement is scary

Retirement is a major development stage involving a great change to your lifestyle. It happens at a time of life when we are not always very receptive to, nor very good at, change. That is scary and the fear that some people feel traps them in a lifestyle they are not enjoying, often working at things that they do not want to be doing any more.

The thing that people are most scared of is using their investment capital to gain income. We do not get very much practice at dealing with lump-sum investment. When we no longer have a payment coming in to our bank account, say every second Thursday, and we are dependent on volatile and capricious markets for the best returns we can get while protecting our capital, it's easy to be fearful about the cost of cheese and visits to the dentist. There are other things to be frightened of, such as the loss of social networks, boredom, health concerns, relationship changes, etc. Nonetheless, the greatest fear is usually about money.

Such financial fears are both intelligent and useful. They are intelligent because reliance on investment markets for returns is uncertain. They are useful because a bit of fear should keep you from investing too aggressively and making big investment mistakes—the promise of high returns usually means high risk. Some humility, even to the point of fear, is a good friend of the retired person as an investor.

When considering how to get over your own 'buts', and thinking about the pitfalls, bear in mind that this change of lifestyle is not, nor should it be, a no-exit street. By this I mean that it should be possible to go back to what you were doing previously if things don't work out. You should not burn any bridges behind you, at least until you are confident that what you are doing is what you want. Therefore, keep up with all your contacts and keep your skills current.

Working less and living more is a change to your lifestyle, but it does not have to be a major dislocation in your life. Your life is a continuum and this is another stage in its development, just as when you look back you can see its earlier stages. It is likely that for some of you the new lifestyle you adopt will not be permanent, and that you will move on to other things.

At sixty, I still don't know what I am going to do when I grow up—I often ask myself that almost youthful question: 'What's next?' I left work, in the sense of going into an office every day, quite a few years ago, and my work for the last few years has been a mixture of writing, presenting workshops, investing and consultancy. However, I think I will probably have another change or two yet, choosing my final career when I consider myself a real grown-up. As I look into my future, I see that I still have one—and it's one that I anticipate with excitement.

3 | A life of two halves

Life, in fact, has many stages or phases—Shakespeare counted seven of them. From a financial or money point of view, however, there are two main stages:

- The first stage is building up your capital, doing what you can to drive up your wealth. This usually happens from your twenties through to your sixties, with the prime time for wealth creation being in your fifties and sixties.
- The second stage is when you go into 'cruise control' and use capital to give yourself income.

That a financial life is in two halves means that, typically, people's net worth goes up in the first half and decreases in the second half. Your focus when you are younger is to make yourself wealthy—buying a house, paying off debt and investing for the future. But, sooner or later, the future arrives and it is time to start to use the wealth that you have built up.

Graphically, this looks like the figure on page 19. This is simply a graph of a typical person's net worth, or wealth, over the course of a lifetime. If you are like most people, you will start at year zero with no wealth. Wealth may build up a little as a teenager, but then become negative as you borrow for your education. Then, in your twenties, thirties and forties, and maybe considerably later, you buy a house, repay debt and invest, and so build up your capital, becoming wealthier. Your net worth is likely to peak in your sixties or seventies, before you ease back and start to use the capital you have for income.

Figure 3.I: A typical person's net worth over a lifetime

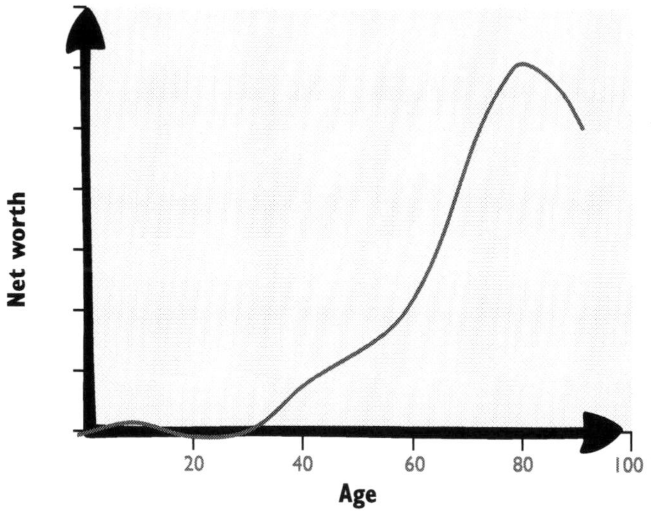

When you look at the graph above, there are more phases than just two. There are the teenage years, the student years, the first years out working, and so on. However, the big financial phases are the years when you build up your wealth, and the years when you start to use your capital. These are the two halves of most lives.

The thing that is hard for most people is the transition from the first to the second half of their financial life. They may have spent thirty years or more managing their money with the aim of building up wealth, and it can be hard to make the change to start spending that wealth. This is a matter of attitude as much as anything else, and it can be difficult to let go of what you have created—to see the capital you worked hard to build up starting to reduce. However, much of the purpose of building up capital is to have it to spend when you work less. People save for their future—it may be hard to admit or accept when it happens, but eventually your future arrives.

Not only is a change of attitude needed, but a change in the types of assets and investments you have is also necessary. The change of attitude comes first—nothing will happen unless you want it to happen and believe that it should happen. When you want to stop building wealth and start to use your capital, you have to rearrange your investments and finances so that you own different things in different proportions.

The purpose of this restructuring and rearrangement is twofold:

- To reduce risk—when you were younger you could afford to carry more risk. In fact, back then you needed to take more risks to get higher returns. There are two ways to reduce risk. First, reduce or, better still, eliminate any debts you might have. Second, diversify more, to spread what you have around a wide range of asset classes and assets. I think many financial advisers take the idea of reducing risk, especially for people who are wanting to ease back or even retire, too far—some financial advisers suggest owning little more than bank deposits and bonds, giving no capital growth and no income growth. This is particularly misguided for people in their fifties and sixties who may spend a long time with limited income from work. These people need some growth assets—shares, property or a business—to keep up with inflation and to give growth of income. Nonetheless, you will need to rearrange your investments to reduce risk as you reach a time in life when you can less afford a major loss.

• To obtain income—while some investments give more income than capital growth, other investments give more capital growth than income. When you start to ease back, you need more income than capital growth. This is what pushes some people towards bank deposits and bonds and away from shares which, as I mentioned above, I think can be a major mistake. You do need growth, and it is possible with some thought to live on capital growth, which is dealt with in Section 3. However, most people will want to see fairly steady income from their investments in the form of interest, rents or dividends.

A useful way to think of the change in the types of assets that you own and how you structure them is to think of the things you own as belonging in one of two categories—they are either Wealth-Creating Assets or Security Assets. These terms were first used in the book *Get Rich, Stay Rich*, published in 2003, that I wrote with Joan Baker. It is useful to divide the assets you might own into these two categories. If your financial life is in two halves, your investments can be structured in two ways to suit the time of your financial life. The trick is to make sure that the right half of your life has the right type of investments.

Wealth-Creating Assets

These are the assets that will make you wealthy because they will give you a high return—my benchmark is that they will grow your wealth by at least 15 per cent per annum. The only assets that can give these sorts of returns are a business, a highly geared property portfolio or an aggressively managed share portfolio. The vast majority of people who have become wealthy have done so through ownership of one of these assets.

The trouble is that although these things will make you wealthy, they are both risky and take up a lot of your time to manage. As such, they are suitable for the first half of your life—the half when you want to build up your wealth. Younger people should own a business, shares or property, and manage them aggressively to build up their capital as quickly as possible. Furthermore, younger people should, by and large, have all their wealth in this area, which means that they are not diversified; that is, they have most of their eggs in one basket. They can afford to do this because they have time on their side. However, as they get older they have less time and want to ease back and, therefore, have to be more careful. Older people, and that is starting to include Baby Boomers, need to have much more of their wealth in Security Assets.

Security Assets

Security Assets are lower-returning investments—but they are also much safer. They are things like the family home once it has become mortgage free, a spread of shares, investment property with low or no mortgage, bank deposits, high-grade bonds, a diversified portfolio across all asset classes, and so on. These are the kinds of assets suitable for people who are a bit older, who cannot afford to take as much risk as when they were younger and who are looking for income. Note that I am not suggesting when you have eased back to a new life everything should be as safe as could be. What I am suggesting, however, is that you will have a lower-risk profile and will, therefore, want to own a quite different set of assets and investments than when you were younger. Security Assets are suitable for the second half of your financial life—when you need to be looking for things that are safer, take less time to manage, and from which you can easily take cash.

Making the transition

Although it is useful to categorise assets and investments as those for the first half of your financial life and those for the second, and to recognise that some are suitable for younger people aggressively building wealth while others are suitable for people who live off their wealth, the division between the two is not really so neat and clear-cut. Nor indeed are the two halves of your life neat and clear-cut. Our parents' generation may have retired neatly at age sixty or sixty-five, so that between one day and the next, everything was different. They stopped work and started living an entirely different lifestyle requiring entirely different finances.

The time is right

It is hard to know when the time is right to start to ease back into a new lifestyle. Generally, I would say that, all else being equal, you should start to make the change to some kind of retirement as early as possible (finances permitting). This is not just because you can enjoy more good summers, but also because at a younger age you will probably adapt more easily to the change. This is partly because we make changes more easily when we are younger but also because the adaptations tend to be smaller.

Some people start to ease back quite early but in doing so they only drop perhaps one day of work each week or, maybe, start to take an extra few weeks as annual holidays. This will obviously depend on your type of work or business and, of course, the earlier you start to do less paid work, the longer you will have to keep working for.

Here is a useful way to think of this: if you are sixty years old, earn $70,000 per annum and plan to retire at sixty-five years, you know that you are going to have $350,000 over the next five years (plus any investment returns). You could decide instead to work half-time and to make up for that, to resolve to work until you are seventy. You will still earn $350,000 plus investment returns but still have the same amount of money over the ten-year period. If you work out the numbers in detail they will not be quite as neat as this, but the idea of working less for longer is a valid way of planning.

Our generation is likely to be quite different. Rather than suddenly stopping work because we have reached some arbitrary age, most of our generation are likely to gradually wind down, perhaps taking a couple of decades to do so. We may start to work less and ease back at the age of fifty-five, but continue to work in some capacity or other through to the age of seventy-five. Your finances may be the same. There is no need to choose a particular day on which you sell your Wealth-Creating Assets and buy into Security Assets. Your life situation is not going to change rapidly and your finances need not either. Your finances should change only gradually, reflecting the lifestyle changes you are making.

An example of this is people who own a business—a typical Wealth-Creating Asset requiring a lot of time and carrying quite a lot of risk. If you simply wanted to retire, you could sell the business on your sixty-fifth birthday, and use the proceeds to purchase Security Assets. Another option, however, is to identify someone who will ultimately own the business, perhaps a family member, a staff member, a supplier or someone else in your industry, and sell a percentage of the business to them. Initially, you may sell, say, 25 per cent of the business to this person—and ideally you would give up some of your management roles to him or her. As time goes on, you can sell more of the business to this person, gradually relinquishing both ownership and management control.

The advantages of doing something like this are:

• You reduce risk as you sell down.
• You continue to get some of the profits from the business, which is likely to be a very good return on your capital.

- You reduce your workload gradually, and you will have reduced responsibility while still having an interest in the business.
- The person who is buying in has time to learn from you and grow into the management role.
- You are not selling everything at the same time, which might not be a good time to sell a business.

Gradually selling down or discontinuing what you are doing works for the other Wealth-Creating Assets too; for example, you can slowly sell some of your aggressive shares, putting the proceeds into a more diversified portfolio of shares, and you can restructure your investment properties, perhaps by selling some and using the proceeds to repay debt on the others you continue to own. This does not need to happen all on one day—in fact, there is every reason why it should happen gradually over a few years.

The key is to have a plan for the transition—to know where you are going and how you are going to get there. Planning for and knowing what you want to own at a certain point in time and working towards it will make the transition a lot easier. Plan for how you are going to move from owning aggressive Wealth-Creating Assets to more passive and less risky Security Assets. You do need to reduce risk—but you do not need to do it overnight. You are moving on to the second half of your life and one day your finances will have to reflect that. To ease back and live the life of your dreams, aim to rearrange your finances and assets to reduce risk and the time that you have to spend caring for things like a business, property or share portfolio.

CHAPTER 4 | Arrange (and maximise) your business

Many people have become wealthy through their businesses. A business, in fact, is probably the most common and effective Wealth-Creating Asset there is. A business is a little bit like a house—it often makes up a large proportion of a family's wealth. A business may be built up over years and decades and can finish up being very valuable—sometimes far more valuable than the owners realise. Some people end up owning a valuable business, a house, and not a lot else. How you handle the business when you make a change in lifestyle—whether you simply sell it and, if you do, at what price, or do something else with it—the decisions you make can make a big difference to how well you enjoy your next twenty summers. You need to think about taking very good advice, and setting a long-term plan for what will become of the business.

When I talk about a business here, I mean a 'real' business. I am not talking about self-employment, about working as a self-employed consultant or tradesman. I mean something that can be sold. A self-employed management consultant might consider himself or herself 'in business', but the reality is that such a person is self-employed and will probably have nothing to sell when the time comes. So, in effect, they are little different from a wage earner or salary worker. The same management consultant could, of course, take on staff, build up a reputation and brand, develop a large and loyal client base and, thus, in the end have something to sell.

Building up a business with value is a very good way to become wealthy, and lots of people have done it very successfully. As such, it is a very good Wealth-Creating Asset, but it is not a good Security Asset. This is because:

- It is a large undiversified asset, and therefore quite risky.
- It is likely to have borrowings.
- It takes up a lot of time—most business owners live, eat and breathe their business, putting a huge amount of time, effort and energy into its development and management.

It is very difficult, but not impossible, to have financial freedom and ease back while you own a business. Your time is not your own, and your money is not your own—businesses frequently have quite high borrowings. It is hard to have passive income from your business. They certainly provide very good active income, but if you want to be less active in the business so that you can do other things you will need passive income.

The first thing you have to recognise is that you will not own the business forever—one day it will either not exist or be owned by someone else. You cannot take a business with you when you die. The question is: who will control the process of succession to someone else, or will it happen in an unplanned, uncontrolled way?

The identification of to whom the business will succeed, and the timing of the succession, is critical for business owners who want to change and live a better lifestyle. This is not something that you want to do on the spur of the moment— it is a process that needs to be planned well in advance.

If you own a business and are ready for a different lifestyle, you have some basic choices—sell the business, put managers in, or sell a part of the business.

Business succession

Business succession is something that may need to be planned over some years. This is particularly so when certain skills and/or qualifications are needed to run the business and there are therefore a limited number of people who can buy in and take over. This is common if the business is in one of the trades or the professions—usually the successor will need to come from that trade or profession.

This may require you to think five years or more ahead and take on staff that will have the aptitude and possible desire to take over. That means instead of hiring juniors, as you might usually, you have to hire intermediate or even senior people who need little training in the technical aspects of their profession or trade, but who you can start to train in management or sales skills.

Selling a business

This is in some ways the most straightforward option. It is simple insofar as you swap the business for an amount of money and you and the business go your separate ways. However, the idea of not owning it can be disconcerting—it represents a major life change. You may worry about how you will spend your time, even if, in all the years of running the business, you have craved more time for yourself. You may also be worried about how you will live without the income that came from the business. This last concern is most easily addressed—you will be swapping the business for some cash that you are going to invest. You are not, after all, going to give the business away. You may need to learn new skills, particularly investment skills, and you will need to adjust to a new lifestyle, but that was what you were wanting! Remember that lots of people have gone before you—you are by no means the first person to have exited a business for a new life.

One thing people often say to me when we are talking about the sale of a business is that they get such good returns from it compared to the income they are likely to get from the sale proceeds. Of course, this is true—you are unlikely to find an investment that will give the same financial returns. However, there are two things that you have to bear in mind:

- Part of the return you get from the business is a return on your time. Many business owners draw a salary to an amount that is efficient for tax purposes, but does not truly reflect what they are worth. When you put a full salary against the profits from the business, the return is not so good.
- Owning a business is risky—many small businesses fail. If you own a business it means you have a great deal of money in one undiversified asset. Moreover, not only is it undiversified, it is also illiquid—you cannot sell it at short notice, as you can with a lot of investments, such as shares. Thus while the returns from businesses are high, so also is the associated risk.

Selling a business is not always easy—you will have to show potential buyers all aspects of it, and things that were previously private and confidential become known to strangers. A client once described this experience as akin to taking off his clothes and standing naked in the local shopping mall! It is something that you should be prepared for well in advance. Buyers must be identified and the business must be in good shape. In my experience, the buyer for your business is likely to be someone who already has some sort of connection to it—a customer, supplier, competitor or staff member. Certainly, you can sell it to some unknown member of the public, but this is often more difficult as you have to start from scratch.

Putting in managers

The returns from your business are likely to be so great that it is tempting to continue owning it, while hiring someone else to manage it. The theory goes that you take a director's or governance role, while a professional manager does the day-to-day work, and you get to choose some interesting aspect to work on while not having to do the daily grind. You also get the higher-income returns.

Although this sounds very good in theory, it frequently does not work out as neatly as planned. Things go wrong in businesses, and when they do, as the owner, you will have to get involved. This may mean that you get called back into management, which may result in your essentially being back in full-time work. Furthermore, you still have all the risks of owning the business. Unless you have other significant assets you will not be well diversified and so will be very exposed financially if things do go wrong. Putting in professional managers and treating your business as if it was some kind of passive investment may be a very tempting idea, but it seldom works out that way. You must be aware that there is plenty that can adversely affect both your financial situation and your lifestyle when things go wrong.

Selling part

This is often my preferred option. It involves selling down a part of the business, and then, all going well, selling more over time, usually to the same person. There are a number of advantages to selling part of a business:

- You continue to receive some of the profits and capital growth of the business—it's likely to be a higher return than you will get from other investments.
- You will not have to be involved in the daily grind, but will still have an overall watch over the business.
- You will have some cash from the sale to pay off debt and to buy some diversified investments.
- It opens the sale up to a wider range of people. If you are selling all of the business, only a limited number of people are likely to have the money and the skills to make the purchase. Selling down a part means that the new part-owner needs less capital and can be trained.
- You are developing someone, perhaps a family member, who will likely become the full owner of the business in time.
- The business may become more successful than it was, as the new owner gives it a new lease of life with his or her energy and different skills and contacts.

- You can help steer the business to a good future with the satisfaction that the business will continue.

There are also some risks and disadvantages, however:

- The new part-owner may not work out. You may end up having to buy him or her out.
- You may have disagreements about the future direction of the business.
- You may find that you are drawn back into the business when problems arise and have to do as much work on it as you ever did.
- You are not wholly free of the business to get on with the other things that you want to do.

The solution to most of these problems is threefold:

- Find the right person.
- Have a good agreement.
- Sell down progressively.

Even if the person you sell to is someone you know, you must have a proper legal agreement drawn up—the same sort of agreement that you would insist on if the party involved were a stranger. Finally, move slowly. Sell perhaps 20 per cent initially, and only sell more if things are still going well in, say, a couple of years. Although your aim may be to sell the entire business, the whole process could take ten years or longer.

It may take you years to completely exit your business. A spur-of-the-moment decision followed immediately by action is likely to leave regrets—less money than you could have got and few ideas about what you are going to do next. The sell down needs to be planned well in advance, with buyers identified and the business prepared. Take your time and take advice. How you arrange your affairs may be the key to how much you can enjoy all those good summers to come.

5 | The importance of work

When I got into the taxi at the airport, the driver immediately recognised me. He had read a book of mine on property and for the thirty-minute drive into the city he had me captive. I like talking to taxi drivers—they know what is going on better than anyone else. He said he had rental property, and asked what I thought of the current market. I guessed he was well into his sixties, and I imagined that he probably had a small flat somewhere and might have been thinking about cashing up.

As we chatted, however, I realised all my assumptions were wrong. He did not own just one property, but six. When I asked if he had his mortgages on fixed rates, he just chuckled and said he had no borrowings. Then he started talking shares—he clearly had a decent-sized portfolio. So I asked the obvious question: 'What are you doing driving this cab? You don't seem to need the money.'

The answer was both simple and complicated at the same time. He had been a factory manager, and when he retired he was so bored after three months that he gratefully accepted the offer to drive his son-in-law's cab. His son-in-law worked nights and my driver drove four fairly short days each week.

It got him out of the house—much to the relief of his wife, who had been forced to ban him from watching Test cricket. He also met people, found out what was going on in the world and, chuckling again, said that every now and then he got some free financial advice. It turned out he was seventy-two, and far from ready to put a shawl over his knees and sit in a rocking chair. No, he didn't need the money, but he did need the focus and the interest of getting out and meeting people, and the feeling of doing something useful. I should have given him a big tip because he had reminded me to stop making easy assumptions about people.

'Work' is a strange word that does not always have good connotations. My dictionary says that it means 'to be occupied by a business or employment'. But it also says that it is 'effort directed to an end'. Mine is an old dictionary, given to me for passing an exam in 1971, but I like that second definition. I don't think that we are wired to do nothing—I think we are wired to strive for something, to put in effort for some kind of end result. We need a goal, and when we reach that goal we need another goal. People without goals of some sort stagnate—with goals we continue to grow and be better.

The problem with work is that we usually think of it as the daily grind—it is what we have done for years, whether it's running a business or answering to a boss. It is what we want to get away from as it has stopped us from being with our families, playing golf, being in the garden or out fishing. We think of it as what we have to do to put bread on the table and this compulsion—the fact that we *have* to do it—makes it very unattractive. But think of the alternative—doing nothing. Even playing golf or being in the garden every day will only go so far. How much fishing or rock climbing can you do?

In any event, experience has shown me that people do want to strive, to put in effort towards a meaningful end.

Even the people I know who are very, very wealthy do not do nothing, nor do they dedicate the rest of their lives towards a lower golf handicap. I have never had a client who has thought that on becoming wealthy they would spend the rest of their days pursuing hobbies and pastimes. And that is another interesting word, pastimes. Why would we want to do things that simply pass the time? Time is, after all, the most valuable thing that we have. Why would we want to do something solely to make our most valuable asset pass more quickly?

You may have only twenty good summers before you reach your three score and ten. There may be things you are burning to do. But these things don't have to preclude work. Whether you take paid work because you need the income, or unpaid work (for example, helping in your community), you are likely to want to strive for something. If it can be unpaid, chances are you will want to do something like mentoring, helping with an aid project or directing a business on an unpaid basis.

If your work has to be paid work, there are options. Do not let all those negative thoughts about work get in the way. It does not have to be the thing that you have done for fifty weeks a year for the last fifteen years. If you have to be in paid work, you are very lucky to be living in the twenty-first century:

- What you know and your experience are now more highly valued than what you can do with your hands.
- There are shortages of all sorts of knowledge workers, including teachers, mentors and instructors.
- There are anti-age discrimination laws.
- Employers are more flexible, allowing for part-time workers.

If you have to work because you need the income, you will have lots of company. The real secret to planning how you are going to live is to think beyond the work you are doing at the moment. What you are doing at the moment may be very unattractive—and you may want to stop. If you think that you can only do what you have always done, you are probably right. But if you think beyond what you have always done, if you think of the skills and the experience you have, you may see that there is a great deal more that you can do. To ease back requires a stocktake of what you want out of life and of what you own. That is why a net worth statement is so useful.

Transition

Making a sudden change from what you are doing now to something different is difficult. We can cope with this when we are younger, but it gets harder as we age.

Years ago, when I was in my twenties, I had a neighbour, Frank, in his early eighties. Frank had been in retirement for over twenty years and used to come over and help me with my garden—he would show me how it should be done. Before he retired, Frank had worked in the same job on the railways for forty years—he was with a gang fixing the tracks and doing fairly hard manual labour.

Frank told me that a couple of years before someone was due to retire, the rail company would move them from the gang and into the workshop to do different jobs. The company had noticed that if someone suddenly went from doing what they had done for decades to retirement they died within two years of stopping work. So, the company started easing its workers into retirement with a small transition by giving them an indoor job. According to Frank, once this happened the workers lived much longer after retirement.

I do not know whether there is any research to support the idea that a sequence of small changes gives better outcomes but, intuitively, it seems right.

You also need to take stock of what knowledge, experience and skills you have. Quite possibly, there is far more than you think. There is not too much that is good about getting older, but one of the good things is the experience you've gained along the way—you will have done a lot of things and have a broad perspective. It may be that you can do something quite different when you start to ease back. You may not have to continue with what you have always done. There may well be something much more interesting and completely different that you can do part time. Your knowledge, skills and experience may cross very easily into other industries and other occupations. It is said that a change is as good as a holiday—if you need to continue to earn income, a change of job might be the break that allows you to stay happy and engaged.

If you are trained in some knowledge area of work, or are able to retrain so that you can become a knowledge worker, you will no longer have to do the physical work, which is harder as we get older. Not only will you be paid more but you will be able to work for longer. Think of it this way—if you are currently earning $50,000 per annum and are planning to work for another five years, you can afford to work part time instead and earn $25,000 per annum for ten years. That is a very attractive idea—it means that you can make changes now, earning income for perhaps half of your time with more time to do the other things that you want with your summers, despite committing to work for longer. This is one of the very good things that the modern world offers us—the ability to keep earning and stay actively engaged in society, while continuing to be usefully and gainfully employed for longer.

I have found that quite often an employer does not want to lose a particularly valued employee, and will bend to accommodate a desired change of lifestyle. One of my clients had been a long-term employee in a middle-management job. The client told his employer that he was planning to leave in the next few months to work part time in a completely different industry. The employer was alarmed at the prospect of losing my client and within a few days offered a role in the business that allowed him to choose his own reduced hours.

I know several people who have tried to resign from senior-management positions in companies based in capital cities because they wanted to move into the country. In each case their employer has bent over backward to accommodate them, allowing them to work from home by email and phone, and to travel into the office as needed—sometimes as little as a couple of times a month. It has to be acknowledged, however, that this sort of arrangement does not always work well—the employee sometimes finds that he or she is travelling a lot and has all the stress they had before, and then some.

Many people are just one skill away from being able to do something quite different. The missing link might be computer skills, sales skills, accounting skills—you name it. A good example of this was a friend of mine who was a builder. In his late forties, he was starting to find scrambling around building sites, putting roofs on houses and carrying heavy loads quite tough. When he learned how to create and use spreadsheets, he found that he was very useful in the office doing pricing and quoting. He could not have done that without the additional computing skills, but a three-week course transformed him from a builder doing heavy work to an office worker in the same industry. In many ways, he was a more useful office worker than most because of his experience and knowledge of the practical side of the industry—he understood the numbers he was working with.

You should treat any course that might help to fill a skill gap as an investment—it may cost a bit of time and money, particularly if it is a longer course taking a year or two, but it will enable you to earn more income for longer. Think about any changes you are going to have to make and the training that you might need as early as possible. Some changes you may need to make have quite a long lead time—you do not want to go cold turkey.

Becoming a consultant can be an option for some. After a lifetime of being employed this might be a bit scary—you have to be very confident that you will be able to find the clients. However, many people leave employment knowing who their clients are going to be—often the main one is their previous employer. Consulting also allows you to work the hours you want. You do need to be careful how you charge for consultancy, however—many people undercharge. Remember that the hours you can charge out are not the same as the hours you have to work: as a self-employed consultant you will have to spend non-billable hours marketing and selling services, putting in systems and looking after the accounts.

You also have to look after your own sick leave, holidays, other down time and costs. This means you should probably charge around double or triple the hourly rate that you were getting as an employee. If you have been earning $30 per hour, you should be charging $60–$90 per hour as a consultant—more if you can get it.

Some people find that they cannot ease back as a consultant—the requirements and strains of being self-employed sometimes turn out to be harder than being employed. Having to get out and sell, pay compliance costs and do things like book-keeping and debt collecting can add up to working at night and at weekends. I have known people who have tried to work less as a consultant but ended up working harder than they had ever done in their lives without earning as much as they used to. For every billable hour you are budgeting for, you will probably spend at least one working hour that you cannot charge. For example, if you need $2,000 per month to make your lifestyle work and you charge out at $100 per hour, you will need twenty billable hours per month. But you will not work only twenty hours per month—it is likely to be nearer forty hours and often considerably more. Being a consultant can be a very good option, but it needs to be planned with a sense of reality.

It's unlikely that you will want to sit around and do nothing—for people who define themselves by what they do, doing nothing means they *are* nothing. Certainly, you will want to spend more time with the family, travelling or engaged in hobbies, but none of these things precludes work. You can work part time, using the income to supplement what you get from investments and superannuation.

Social status

Retirement brings many changes. The changes to how you define yourself and how others treat you are among the greatest. Sarah's experience of retirement made this clear to me.

Sarah had been an employment lawyer with a fairly large law firm and she had a high profile within the profession. A couple of weeks after she retired she was at a social function and was asked what she did. For the first time, she gave her occupation as retired. Sarah noted how her questioner's eyes immediately darted around the room looking for someone more interesting to talk to and how he soon found an excuse to move off to another group.

Saying you are retired does not sound very exciting to a lot of people, so it may pay to redefine yourself. This could be according to work you do for a charity or, perhaps, as I suggest to many of my clients, you may start to think of yourself as an investor.

The negative connotations of work are as much a state of mind or an attitude as anything else. You may want a break between leaving your full-time job or selling a business. Your plans to ease back can very easily include some income from employment. Think creatively—the skills that you have will cross over into other areas and other occupations. You can drive a taxi, be a consultant, do the accounts for some small businesses, teach organic gardening, restore cars, do flower arrangements for reception desks, coach maths to earn money, and still have the time to do the things you have always wanted to do.

6 | The 'enough is never enough' syndrome

People overestimate how much wealth they will need to live comfortably on their investments. I have seen it over and over again—many people think they need a lot more capital to fund their lifestyle than they actually need. The 'enough is never enough' syndrome has you always looking for more capital, and always feeling that you never have quite enough to change to the life you want to live. You may be a lot closer to freedom than you think. There are probably three things driving this syndrome:

- Feelings of insecurity—these are rational enough, in that we are biologically programmed to work to ensure we do not run out of the wherewithal of life. The basic fear that our money will run out before we do can drive us to keep working, keeping on building up our wealth far beyond our true needs.
- The industry that encourages us all to save more and to keep on saving—I see many professional advisers and commentators frightening people into saving by suggesting that you need bigger amounts of saving than I think are really necessary. Far be it for me to encourage less saving

and investing. After all, I have made a career out of helping people to do so, but I do think a dose of realism about your actual needs for retirement is appropriate.

- Fear of change—fearful of changing their lives, some people keep on working or running their businesses, telling themselves they do not yet have enough. This is clearly an excuse so the person does not have to make changes to their life and lifestyle. I have no problem with people not wanting to change if they are happy with their lives. But when people who are saying they don't have enough when, with a bit of planning or reorganising they really do, are also saying that they are sick of their work or their business, I do see a problem.

Many of the people who say they don't have enough, or who set a very high estimate of how much they need, have never done any kind of exercise to plan how they would use their capital to live on as income. Nor have they ever made any kind of calculation to work through the numbers. Their assessment of how much they need is based on a number they have simply plucked out of the air—the 'think of a number and double it' approach to financial planning. You may never be able to make an exact calculation of how much you need and you should always add a bit more than the numbers suggest, to make quite certain you will have enough, but that should not stop you doing at least a few basic numbers and estimates. Section 2 of this book is designed to help you make this calculation.

The reality is that calculating the amount of capital you need to retire is difficult and has many different factors. Many of these factors are personal to you and concern how much paid work you are prepared to do, whether you want to leave an inheritance for your children or grandchildren, and your investment strategy. I find that many people do, indeed, have enough if they are prepared to make some important decisions and compromises. There is wisdom gained and a better life to be had in being able to say that you have enough—that you do not have to keep striving for more. You could be a lot closer to freedom than you think—indeed, you may already be there.

7 | Risks to your twenty good summers

Not everyone gets a wonderful twenty good summers. There are plenty of people who do not manage the transition very well from full-time work or running their own business to some kind of retirement. Bad stuff does happen, and it happens to people in retirement just as much as to others. When it does happen to people in retirement, it really happens—disasters are much harder to recover from later in life.

Problems that arise in retirement are often financial, and they are the big, obvious ones. However, difficulties also arise socially and within families. If adjustments are not made, disaster in one form or other may beckon. Although some of these things are well outside my area of expertise, I have seen enough to know that there are dragons and where some of those dragons live.

This chapter aims to get you to think about what risks you face and how you can avoid or mitigate them so you are not living your life continually worrying about the bad things that might happen. There is a misery in excessively worrying about an event that may or may not happen that is just about as bad as the event itself. Instead, I am just pointing out some of the common risks on the basis that forewarned is forearmed.

Psychologists point to studies that show that you are more likely to survive a plane crash if you do nothing more than consciously note where the nearest exit door is on the aircraft as you take your seat. This small pre-flight precaution does not mean that you need to spend the entire flight with your teeth gritted and your hands clamped to the seat, white knuckles shining. However, turning your mind briefly to the idea that bad stuff happens and what you might do if it does is a very simple way of improving your survival chances. So, it pays to think about what might go wrong—the stakes are high, but not so high as a plane crash!

This is especially so when it comes to financial and investment management where you need to find the sweet spot between taking too much risk and too little. Too much risk will mean that eventually you will not be able to tolerate the volatility. Sure, over long periods of time a portfolio with a lot of shares will give the best returns. However, the volatility will most likely mean that at some point during a market crash you will end up selling out into that crash, which is exactly when you are not meant to do. Too little risk on the other hand might mean that your returns are so poor that your portfolio struggles to keep up with inflation, let alone giving you a decent return so that you can live well.

If you have to err on one side or the other, later in life it is better to err on the cautious side of the investment spectrum. In particular, be very wary of trying to play catch-up. People starting to eye up some good summers can do little to greatly enhance their financial position—they can only really mess it up and wreck their lives, especially if they push for higher returns.

It pays to remember that the vast majority of investment literature is aimed at younger people trying to build wealth.

These people have different financial profiles and, therefore, different investment plans. As you plan for your good summers beware of following advice that is aimed at younger people. I expect, as more and more Baby Boomers start to use their investment capital to live on, there will be more investment advice aimed at them. In the meantime, however, as you read investment plans ask the question, 'Is this aimed at me?'

Most people fear that their money will run out before they do, but I have never really known this to happen. Unless there is some kind of major mistake or market crash, the money does not simply run out because most people become more cautious with age and take fewer risks with their money.

More commonly, it is the lifestyle that runs out. People cut their expenditure when investment returns are poor rather than simply carrying on spending at the higher level and running down their investment capital. Reducing expenditure is not much fun, of course, but provided there was a reasonable investment approach adopted this would generally only be temporary.

The investment sweet spot with the right amount of risk giving the right amount of return does exist, but it will be different for each of us and getting a happy fit between you and your investments is the critical part of portfolio design. Risk and return need to be balanced and, like Goldilocks, you want it just right.

So, let's look at the various risks that you have which might stop you enjoying your twenty good summers:

1. Your income stops

As suggested above, this is unlikely to be permanent unless you have some eccentric investment strategy; for example, if you had all your investment capital in just one or two properties and were planning to live on the rents it is quite conceivable that income will stop when you lose a tenant. Depending on the kind of property, it may be difficult to sign up new tenants and this could see you without a means to pay for the groceries for quite a long time. Similarly, people who continue to own their business, perhaps with managers looking after it, are also quite exposed if they do not have other funds invested elsewhere.

Even people who have a more conventional investment strategy can lose their income or part of it. The benefits of a diversified portfolio, however, are that you are unlikely to lose all of your income and the loss is not likely to be permanent. Actually, periods of low investment returns should be expected and planned for by always holding some cash as outlined in Chapter 20.

2. Inflation

The big market crashes and losses from fraud make the headlines and everyone feels sorry for people whose lives have been wrecked by a financial crash or a widespread scam. However, more money is probably lost by the insidious effects of inflation. Inflation does not usually steal money in big headline-grabbing chunks, but does it surreptitiously with few people noticing. It nibbles away at investments as it erodes capital and income.

Given that you may be retired for a long time, inflation is one of your greatest risks. For example, you may be taking $20,000 per annum from your investment capital and you may get this amount of money reliably for ten years. However, even at an inflation rate of just 2 per cent, in ten years' time, the spending power of that $20,000 has been eroded to about $17,000. Similarly with your capital, if you buy a ten-year bond worth $20,000, it is likely that in ten years' time the issuer will give you your $20,000 back. However, it will not be the same as the $20,000 you invested because it will only have the buying power of $17,000 from the time you made the investment.

This means that if you want to maintain the real value of your investment capital, you have to grow the amount of investment capital in line with inflation. To do this, you cannot take all the investment returns that you get and spend them. You need to put some back into the investment fund to keep it growing. You will, therefore, need some investments that give a higher return; that is, shares and property, to allow you to draw reasonably on your investment capital but still leave enough there so that your capital will grow.

3. Scams

Many people's lives are wrecked by scams. It never ceases to amaze me how many people fall for scams and that many of the people who do are by no means silly but quite sophisticated. Scams have three main features:

- They offer very high returns.
- The promoters will always suggest urgency—you have to do it now, the opportunity will not last so there's no time to ask advisers about it.
- The minimum amount keeps falling—if the minimum amount is $20,000 and you do not bite, they will offer

a half share at $10,000 and then, if that doesn't work, a quarter share at $5,000.

There is a bit of a blurred line between outright scams and some investment schemes—an offer may not have started out with the intention of scamming but desperation pushes the organisers into it. Most Ponzi schemes are like this. Nevertheless, most also play on the greed of the victims. Always remember, you are unlikely to be able to significantly enhance your financial position when you are getting older, but you can certainly mess it up.

4. Complete global meltdown

I do not think the planet is likely to go back to the Dark Ages of plague, pestilence, the breakdown of the rule of law, collapse of paper currencies and widespread famine. However, there is always a chance, if not of complete meltdown, then of something which is pretty bad. Diversification, especially geographic diversification, is the key to withstanding something like this and, so, many people think owning some gold will see them through.

I own a bit of gold—a few gold coins that I keep to hedge against complete economic and currency meltdown. Some people say that paper (fiat) currencies will not last and that eventually the world will have to return to currencies based on gold. While I doubt that, they just may be right, so I hedge that risk by owning a few gold coins.

Note, however, that I do not consider gold to be an investment. An investment has to give an income return, like shares, property and interest-earning deposits. I do not try to make money from gold—that is speculation, not investment. Instead, I hold some solely as a hedge against hyper-inflation and the collapse of currencies.

5. Major events

There are things like fires, storms, and earthquakes that destroy property and businesses, most of which are insurable. However, there are plenty of people who have suffered losses in such events and find that they are not fully insured. The mitigation of risks of this sort is simply the diversification of what you own—diversification across asset classes, across individual investments and geographical diversification. After one of these types of events, you do not want to find that it was a poor idea to have all your assets in the town in which you live.

6. Health

With the rapid improvement of medical science, there will be more procedures and treatments to keep you well and alive for longer. You should make provision for this, perhaps by continuing private medical insurance or, more likely, by putting aside a lump sum specifically for healthcare. Ideally, this would be a lump sum that is invested in fairly liquid investment so that you can get at it quickly if need be, but only when you really need it for healthcare.

7. Boredom

More than once, I have got into a taxi that is driven by a retired professional of some sort who clearly does not need the money. Instead, the driver has retired and got bored and, so, has gone back to some kind of work. This is fine provided that what they go back to is not a fairly major business of some kind. A taxi is not going to require too much capital. It is a whole different ball game if a bored retiree buys a bigger business or perhaps, more commonly, funds a family member into one with the idea that the retiree will work a bit in the business to share the benefit of his or her wisdom—whether it's wanted or not.

People do all sorts of weird things when they get bored and sometimes wreck their lives in the process. Sure, you may have run a successful business for decades, but in retirement you need to be careful about putting too much money into something that may not work out.

Section | 2

Setting things up

CHAPTER 8 | Do we have enough?

The title of this chapter says it all. It is a question that many of us ask ourselves when we want to step back and have an easier lifestyle, but we also want to start doing the things we have always promised ourselves we will do 'sometime'. Years of trying to get ahead financially have created an ingrained habit of striving for more savings and investments but the time comes, perhaps in our forties, fifties or sixties, when we ask ourselves: Have we made it? Do we have enough?

It is really one of the fundamental questions of human existence. We expect a future—hopefully a future that will span more than twenty summers—and we want that future to be secure. Change is always difficult, and the sort of change to your means of support that you may be contemplating can be downright frightening.

The answer to the question 'Do we have enough?' is not straightforward. For most of us, it is not simply a matter of looking at how much we have in savings and investments and working out an answer on a calculator. There are eight major factors or variables that have to be looked at and considered separately and in relation to each other—their balance has to be played with and adjusted for everyone until there is an answer suited to each person's hopes for their future life and lifestyle. As decisions are made you will create a plan that will let you build a new, more relaxed and more peaceful lifestyle with financial comfort.

The eight main factors you need to take account of in developing a plan to reduce your dependency on paid work and to have more time are:

- The amount of capital you have
- The lifestyle you want
- The house you want
- Whether you want to leave an inheritance for your children
- The extent to which you will continue paid work, and for how long
- Any other income you have
- Your age and how long you expect to live
- Your investment returns.

Each of these eight factors is dealt with in detail in this section. Suffice to say here that unless you have a quite high net worth and, therefore, a lot of capital available to invest, it is likely that you will have to alter your expectations of some factors and continue to readjust them until you get a plan that gives you the amount of money you need to fund a lifestyle acceptable to you. For example, it may be that you want to work only three days a week for another five years, and then stop work completely. This may have the result that your income will be too little later on, unless you trade off one of the other factors; for example, you might reduce the lifestyle you want, downsize your house or, perhaps, decide to leave a lesser inheritance to the kids.

Life is all about compromise—none of us can have absolutely everything that we want. You are starting to plan for a new phase in your life—it should be an exciting process for an exciting new life. However, the plan will probably not fit together neatly at first—you will have to compromise on some factors and trade off between other factors. In other words, you will have to rank the factors and decide which of the eight factors are more important to you than the others—which can you give up on and still be quite happy? This process is almost inevitable for all but the wealthiest people and people with extremely modest needs.

The answer to the question 'Do we have enough?' is part calculation, part judgment—or part science, part art. The calculation side works for some of the eight factors discussed; for example, how much income you need for your lifestyle, and how much capital you have at the moment. Other factors are a matter of judgment; for example, how long you are likely to live, and how much longer you will enjoy doing some paid work. You will never be able to answer these questions precisely—you have to make some guesses. You are making a plan for the future and few plans for the future ever work out neatly and follow the script.

Moreover, as you look at each factor you may well have to adjust some of the things you want less so you can have the things you want more. This is not a plan where you can make all the pieces of the puzzle fit and stay fitted for all time. Rather, it is a plan of continual decision-making and trading off one item against others.

And so back to the question: Do we have enough? What capital do you need to be able to do less, including earning less, and still have the confidence that the money will not run out and you will not have to spend your last days in poverty or penury? How much do you need to enjoy freedom? Do you have enough? When we have WealthPlanning clients, one of the first things we do is help them establish what we call their Freedom Figure—the amount of money they will need in order to live off their capital in comfort and with some confidence that they can enjoy the lives of their dreams. With WealthPlanning, the Freedom Figure becomes the goal the client is working towards—it is the amount of net worth needed to fund the lifestyle they want into the future.

The Freedom Figure obviously varies from individual to individual, but the amount of money required to be free is very often a lot less than people realise. Often, clients who say they want to increase their wealth discover, when we do this exercise, that they already have enough! These clients don't need to increase their incomes and their wealth at all because they are already in a position to start enjoying the lives of their dreams.

Generally, I work on the Freedom Figure—the amount of investable capital you will need—as being approximately twenty times the amount of the after-tax income you need. This is a very rough rule of thumb, but means that if you wanted before-tax income of $50,000 per annum you would need around $1,000,000 of investable capital. There are ways and means of freeing up the capital you need, whether from your house, your business or from your investments, so that you can apply that capital to income-producing assets which will allow you to live a life of freedom.

This is an exercise that you will have to do—to have the freedom to take maximum advantage of the next twenty summers, you need to know how much capital you need to generate the income returns required.

Investment returns

Working out your likely investment returns is a very difficult process. First, you have to consider what your gross investment returns will be. This will depend on your asset allocation; that is, how much you will have in each of the main asset classes of shares, property, bonds, and cash. The returns that you will get before tax will be the total returns—both income and capital growth—and they will be calculated over a long period of time. Just because the long-run rate of return for a particular portfolio is 8 per cent does not mean that each and every year you will get 8 per cent.

Second, the gross returns will be taxed. This also is a difficult calculation as capital gains are taxed differently from income. Moreover, some investments are taxed differently from others and tax rules tend to change quite a lot. You will need to make an intelligent guess at your overall tax rate.

Third, if you want to retain the real inflation-adjusted value of your capital you will need to think about what inflation will be over the coming decades. This is impossible to predict accurately, but I usually work on 2 per cent.

There is quite a lot that may prove to be inaccurate in making this calculation, but you do need to try it to see if you are close to being able to ease back.

Few people live entirely on income derived from their investments. If you want to step down from full-time work to enjoy more fully some good summers, you do not have to plan to live solely from your investment capital. Many people would find they simply do not have enough to do so, and thus would have to stay at the grindstone for many years yet.

The income you need does not solely depend on how much capital you have. There are other factors at play; for example, the extent to which you will continue to work, or other income you might have. The plan you develop needs to take account of them all.

It is quite possible that you already have enough and it's just that you feel less financially secure than you really are. Many of my clients simply have feelings that stop them making the changes in their lives they say they want to make. Quite often they have not done the numbers, not started to do any sort of planning, and not thought through how they would live if they reduced their working—earning—lives in some way. My conclusion is that people often feel more comfortable keeping on doing what they do, even when they say they want to stop doing it. It is often easier to keep on with the habits of a lifetime than to make changes, even if they would help move you towards something that is likely to be better. Change can be very difficult.

The farmer, the chickens and the eggs

The distinction between income and capital is critical to understand. In Accountancy 101 they teach that capital is the tree and income is its fruit. I prefer to think of capital as a chicken and income as an egg. The egg (income) is derived from the chicken and provided that you do not eat the egg

---

it will grow to become another chicken and eventually start to produce even more eggs. Similarly, you could eat the chickens (capital) that you have, but if you do this, they will not produce as many eggs (income).

Think of a chicken farmer who does nothing else but run his farm of thousands of laying chickens. Clearly the farmer will live on the eggs that his chickens produce. Provided that he has enough chickens laying eggs for him he can consume some of the eggs and keep some to replace his laying stock. If he has enough chickens laying enough eggs to give him good nutrition and to replace the chickens that will inevitably die or stop laying, all will be happiness. He has a sustainable chicken farm off which he can live happily (albeit a bit boringly—all those eggs and nothing else).

However, if he does not have enough chickens laying enough eggs to sustain him he has to think of some others ways to get by and feed himself. One of those options would be to leave the chickens to themselves for a couple of days a week and get a job on a neighbour's chicken farm (where he would be paid in eggs, of course). The eggs from his own chickens and those from working for his neighbour part time ought to be enough to sustain him. It might even be that he has a small surplus and can keep a few eggs to hatch into chickens and so one day have a farm which is completely self-sustaining.

The other option would be to supplement his diet of eggs by killing and eating a few chickens. Long term, of course, this is not sustainable—the more chickens you kill and eat, the fewer eggs you are going to have. However, long term it is possible that living in part off eggs (income) and in part off chickens (capital) is an option (provided that you get the timing right and the chickens do not run out before you do).

The real point of all this is that if you are planning to live more and work less, your objective is much less likely to be the building up of a big flock of chickens than finding a way of producing more eggs for consumption. I am no expert on chicken farming, but it seems likely to me that the type of chicken you will need to produce eggs for consumption will be a different breed from the chickens you will need to produce eggs for breeding and building up a flock. This is certainly the case in investment—the types of investment assets that you own for income will be quite different from those you have for capital growth.

As well as this, remember that you do have the option of living off capital if you need to. This is effectively supplementing your diet by killing some chickens. It is not sustainable long term but it could keep you going for the time that you need it. In any event, in the long term you will not need the chicken farm—you won't be able to take it with you. In the meantime, you can enjoy a great diet (and life) living off your capital stock.

The next eight chapters look one by one at the factors already discussed that you need to consider when trying to answer the question 'Do we have enough?'

9 | Factor one: how much capital do you have?

To answer the question 'Do we have enough?', the first thing you need to know is how much you already have. How much capital you have is the starting point for any plan you make for your future lifestyle and freedom. In financial terms this means taking a snapshot of what you have. You could see this as doing a stocktake—looking at what you own or your assets, and deducting what you owe or your liabilities—to get a picture of your net worth. Looking at your net worth is one of the most important parts of planning for your freedom. Before making any plans, you need to know what you have to work with.

For many people, the use of income from savings and investments to help fund a new lifestyle will be a critical part of the plan. To be free, you need your investments to provide income. In some cases this will be the only income you have to live on, for others it will supplement income from other sources. Investing for income to help pay the bills will, no doubt, be a significant change from the way you have previously invested—you will stop trying to build up wealth, instead finding ways to maximise the income from the wealth you already have and using that income to live. A strategy for wealth creation is necessarily quite different from one that seeks to maximise income, so your money will now be invested in different areas. Using the capital you have built to derive income may mean breaking the habits of a lifetime, something that is never easy to do.

Clearly, the more capital you have, the more income you will have. You can supplement your income by living off capital, but that will have a time limit. You could also continue to build up your capital, but that is likely to mean working more than you might wish.

Your net worth is all your saleable assets—what you own that could be turned into cash—minus your liabilities—what you owe. As such, it is your total available capital.

A typical net-worth statement would look like this:

	Dollar value	Totals
Assets (+)		
House	$450 000	
Business	$350 000	
Shares	$75 000	
Investment property	$300 000	
		$1 175 000
Liabilities (−)		
Business debt	$125 000	
Property mortgage	$75 000	
		$200 000
Net worth		$975 000

There are a number of things to note with this net-worth statement:

- Items like cars, boats and furniture are not included. These things depreciate over time and are, therefore, really value-losers. In any event, it is very unlikely that you would ever want to sell these things, as they are needed for lifestyle purposes. An exception to the rule would be cars that are collector's items and, similarly, with furniture antiques that were purchased as 'investments' that you would be happy to sell to help fund lifestyle costs.

- The house is included. Although you are likely to want to keep the house to live in, it should be considered 'in play' because you could decide to downsize or upgrade it or maybe, even, move into rental accommodation. It may be that to live the life you want you are planning to move to another town or neighourhood. It may also be that you decide to use some home-equity release product or reverse-equity mortgage, effectively borrowing against the house to obtain income. This is discussed in Chapter 11. Whatever happens, there is usually so much capital tied up in a house that it has to be considered in play.

- Any business is entered at market value, not net asset value. This means that you add on to the value of the business's assets things like goodwill, licences and so on, so that you enter a true amount—what you would actually get if you sold the business. What you would actually get for the business if you decided to sell it can be very hard to establish, but it does need to be attempted. It is hard to be free while you still have a business to run, thus, you need a reasonably accurate idea of how much capital you would free up by selling up. A call to your accountant may be in order here.

- Liabilities should be established as the amount it would cost to repay all loans in full at this time. This will vary depending on whether a loan involves revolving credit; for example, an overdraft, or repaying principal. Call your lender to establish the amounts required.

Your net worth is the size of your bank account if you sold everything, repaid all debt and put the balance in the bank. There is a useful way to think of this: if you decided to have a completely new life in another country and sold up everything before you went, how much would you have? This is looking at your life from the point of view that everything is possible (as indeed it is). It is important to ascertain, as best you can, your net worth at this point—you cannot know whether you have enough to be free if you do not know how much you have.

You have achieved your Freedom Figure if you have enough capital—a large enough net worth—to produce the passive income you need to live the life you want.

If you do not seem, at first glance, to have enough net worth, do not despair! There are ways and means that might make the life of your dreams possible, if not today, then in the not-too-distant future—variables can be changed, adjusted and readjusted. Remember that how much capital you have is only one factor or variable of the eight in our reckoning. Certainly, it is one of the most important because if you had millions in savings and investments you could almost certainly step back from your work today and live an easier life tomorrow. However, even if you have relatively modest capital you should look at the other seven factors to see if there is a way to rearrange your finances for a better life.

10 | Factor two: the lifestyle you want

Lifestyle is one of the main factors you can work with and adjust to make sure you will have enough when you stop full-time work. In some ways this chapter title is wrongly worded: 'the lifestyle you want' should perhaps be 'the lifestyle you *can reasonably expect*'. You might want a life with a villa in Tuscany, big boats, long holidays in St Moritz and the Caribbean, a Learjet . . . but very few people can realistically expect these things and that lifestyle, and even fewer end up having it. So, the lifestyle you might want can be quite different to the lifestyle that seems reasonable. You probably already have a fair idea of the lifestyle that will be within your reach—it is unlikely to be the opulent one described above, but nor is it likely to be mean and poor, living in a small hut in the bush. Somewhere between those two extremes will be the lifestyle that you can reasonably expect for the next twenty or more good summers.

Your job now is to cost this lifestyle. How much money is it going to take on a weekly, monthly or annual basis to fund it? This is a critical part of the exercise, because you can never answer the question 'Do we have enough?' if you don't know what it will cost you to live and do the things you want to do.

Your lifestyle is clearly one of the things you can alter if the answer to the question is negative. Costing our lifestyle and adjusting expenditure so that it is within our means is what most of us have done all our lives.

It is likely that the lifestyle you expect will have a fairly close relationship to the lifestyle you have now and that your expenditure will remain about the same as it has been in the years leading up to your decision to work less and play more. Some people have a very clear idea of how much they spend to live, others are less clear about it. You may have lived to a budget and stuck to it very closely for years or you may have spent money as it came in. Wherever you sit on what is a very wide spectrum of spending patterns, it is going to be critical as you plan the next phase of your life that you know what it will cost to fund your new lifestyle.

The amount you have been living on up until now becomes the baseline or starting point for calculating what it is going to cost to fund your future lifestyle. But remember, it is only a starting point—there will be changes to your lifestyle and therefore changes to your expenditure.

It has been calculated that, on average, retired people live on 70 per cent of the amount that they lived on before retirement. Expenditure often changes for people in retirement for a range of reasons; for example, less clothing expenses as good work clothes are no longer required, less travel costs as many couples in retirement only have one car, discounts for senior citizens, etc.

However, you are not going into retirement. You need, therefore, to be very careful about this 70 per cent figure. Applying it to your current expenditure would be dangerous—it is likely to be inaccurate for a range of reasons, including the following:

- You are *not* retiring and your lifestyle is likely to be quite different from a retired person's.
- Because you are likely to continue to work to some degree, transport and clothing costs may not fall.
- The 70 per cent is what financial advisers use as an average, but there are many unders and overs.
- You may have higher expenditure in the hobby/sports category; for example, I have enough climbing gear in the garage to fully equip at least three simultaneous Everest expeditions!
- You may be planning to travel a lot.

The 70 per cent rule may be accurate later as your expenditure probably will fall over the years, but it is not necessarily accurate for people just starting to slow down and ease back from work to make the most of the good summers they have before them. Instead of simply applying an average, blanket percentage reduction to your expenditures, you should do a new budget, trying to factor in all the aspects of the new life you are planning to have, costing each activity as accurately as you can. Of course, you will not get this perfectly right first time—no budget or plan for the future works out exactly—but as time goes on you can revise and refine your figures. More important than getting this plan for expenditures exactly right is having a realistic idea of what your new life is going to cost so that you can decide whether or not you are going to have enough.

Therefore, do not sweat the small stuff unduly. The purpose of doing this budget at this stage is to see whether you already have enough, and whether what you have, and the income you can generate, will fund a lifestyle that is sufficiently attractive to you. This budget will show what things you might have to cut from your planned lifestyle or what things you will be able to add to it. Without doing some kind of expenditure budget, you will never be able to answer the question 'Do we have enough?' with any confidence.

The table below is an example of how to work through a budget category by category. This exercise forces you to think about how you are going to live and the money you are going to spend.

Category	Current expenditure p.a.	Future expenditure p.a.	Note
Groceries	$10 000	$10 000	Unlikely to change
Car costs	$6000	$4000	Sell one car
Overseas travel	$0	$6000	One trip each year
Clothing	$6000	$4000	Less work clothes needed
Hobbies	$3000	$6000	More garden expenditure and travel for fishing and golf
House maintenance	$3000	$500	Do more ourselves

If your expenditure budget works out well within the income you are likely to have, you can relax. Go ahead now and have the life that you want. But if there is a deficit, or if the budget looks very tight, you have two options:

- Cut some things out of your plan—lower your expenditure and therefore your lifestyle. We all have to do this to some extent or other—no one can have absolutely everything they want. However, there does come a point where you have to cut out so much that the whole exercise becomes marginal and you can see yourself living in that little hut in the bush. If this is the case you have a second option.

* Look at the other seven factors and see which of them you could adjust to make the plan work. For example, you might decide to work an extra month a year, or to downsize the house to give you more investment capital and, therefore, more income. This is the trading off that everybody has to do to some extent or other, whether they realise it or not.

I cannot stress enough that looking at your likely future expenditure levels is not about living a poor, mean, miserable little life. You are going through this process at this early stage so you can make a plan that will give you the confidence that you will have enough for the rest of your life. You want to go into your new life with a feeling of security, and knowing how much this life will cost is a key part of the plan.

Healthcare

This is likely to be a major expense for which you will have to budget. The advances that are being made in medical science mean that we should be able to live better for longer.

Many more good summers are becoming possible as biotech research provides breakthroughs, new surgical procedures are developed and we have new and improved pharmaceuticals. Perhaps the most exciting of all of these are stem-cell therapies, which hold immense promise for the treatment of a range of conditions.

However, this bright new and longer future comes at a cost in a variety of ways:

- First, the treatments that become available may need to be paid for directly by you.
- Second, living better for longer means that you will have to plan to spend more money in retirement.
- Third, as the Baby-Boomer cohort ages, the expense to governments becomes greater and this may result in a lowering of a range of public services.

Some people plan for this expected additional healthcare cost by putting aside a part of their investment capital and dedicating it to healthcare. Others resolve to continue their health insurance or simply increase their budgeted amount for health. However you decide to do it, it is probably a good idea to plan for spending more on healthcare in retirement than you would have thought necessary in the past.

11 | Factor three: the house you want

The house you want is really part of expenditure for the lifestyle you want, but it deserves its own separate chapter because a house is such a big part of most people's finances. In fact, most people have the bulk of their wealth tied up in their houses.

In their twenties and thirties quite a lot of couples adopt the 'bigger house' financial strategy. This involves buying a house, paying down the mortgage until it has gone—or at least is greatly reduced—and refinancing to buy a bigger house. Over the course of two or three decades the process is repeated several times, meaning that the couple end up with a very big, very valuable house, but usually not much else. The idea is that later in life they will sell the big expensive house and downsize to something smaller and less expensive. The money left over is to be invested and used for retirement.

There is a lot wrong with this strategy from a financial or investment point of view, including no diversification and no exposure to offshore share markets. But the biggest thing wrong with it is that people who have lived in a big expensive house are often very reluctant to downsize simply because they have hit the magical age of sixty-five and decided to retire. People who have had years living in a nice house with all the extras are not at all keen on giving up all the space, the garden and the swimming pool!

Even if you did not adopt the 'bigger house' strategy consciously and deliberately when younger, you may well find yourself caught in much the same bind—most of your wealth is tied up in your house. This becomes very apparent when you do a net-worth statement, as discussed in Chapter 9, and find that in the asset column there is a house with a very big number beside it and not a lot else.

The house is often the most valuable chip that you have to play with and, sometimes, to have enough to slow down and work less it may have to be sold. In any event, in the planning stage when you are asking the question 'Do we have enough?', you have to include your house. For the Freedom Factor assessment to work you have to consider all eight factors, and this is likely to be one of the biggest. Some will have enough without needing to sell the house or do anything else with it, but many will not. At first, doing something with the house might not seem an attractive option, but it might become more attractive than adjusting one of the other factors; for example, living a less expensive lifestyle, perhaps by travelling less than planned. Thinking about how you might access some of the capital in the house might also prove to be more attractive than simply abandoning the whole idea of living the next twenty summers as you would like! You have to think of the house as being in play.

So, how might you use the house to help you have enough to live the life you want with less time at the office? Following are some of the options.

Borrow on the house using some kind of annuity mortgage

Annuity mortgages—also known as home-equity release—are very popular in Europe, and are now available in most countries. These products vary considerably, but the basic premise is that they allow you to draw on the equity in your home by borrowing while you are still living in the home. The interest on the borrowings you make is not usually required to be paid in cash by you, but is added to the total amount owing. When the house is sold or when you die, the total amount you have borrowed—the principal and the interest accrued—is repaid. You can usually borrow to a total of around 50–60 per cent of the house's value. These products are a little like being able to eat your cake while having it, too. They are very suitable for older people but less so for people in their forties, fifties and sixties because the longer they run the more interest is owed, and so you can draw less for living. Another thing you have to realise is that if you nibble away at the house's equity as you continue to live in it, there will be less inheritance for the children when you die, as discussed in Chapter 12.

Sell the house and buy something less expensive

This is the obvious thing to do, but you have to be able to overcome the pain of selling a house that perhaps you like very much and are used to. The idea itself is simple—you buy something cheaper and the capital that you have freed up is invested to generate income. The negative, of course, is that you no longer own what may well have been a lovely house with all the features and facilities you were so fond of. But the cheaper house may be no less attractive; for example, the reduction in price may come from its location. Many people in the last few years have sold their house in a major city and moved out to a nearby country area. Others have sold up and moved to a small town on the coast or in the mountains although, partly because of this trend, these are becoming quite expensive. Because you are unlikely to be working full time, living an hour or so out of a city is much less of a problem than if you need to go into the office every day. Furthermore, a new life often involves working different hours, so that the drive into the city may be outside peak traffic times. If living outside the city is not your idea of bliss, apartment living may be an option—apartments are often significantly cheaper than houses on large sites.

Find a way to derive income from the house

It may be that you can take in a boarder, or convert part of the house into a self-contained flat that can be rented. It may be that you have grown-up children who have descended on you, again, and could quite reasonably be asked for board. Most people I know who travel for extended periods let their houses, coming back to several thousand dollars of accumulated rent.

Subdivide

Quite a lot of people with houses on large blocks of land are able to subdivide the land. While this can free up quite a lot of capital, it may be unattractive because you will now have a new house very close by. It may be more palatable to subdivide and build on the new section yourself, thus having control over the new building. You can then either sell the new house—hopefully making a good profit—or keep it and rent it out, thereby retaining some control over the new neighbours.

Reduce housing costs

There may be cost reductions that you can make concerning the house. Working less ought to mean that you can do a lot more around the house yourself; for example, you may no longer need a housekeeper or gardener, and you may be able to look after the swimming pool and undertake other maintenance yourself.

Clearly, you need to think very hard about what you will do with the house when you start to live your new life—there is usually too much capital tied up in it to ignore. Some people hold on to their very nice house, in spite of the large amount of capital it represents, because they can easily afford to. Others who can only just afford to hold on to it do so because, with its garden and swimming pool, they regard it as not just a place to live but as their hobby and it is very attractive to the children and grandchildren as well.

If the answer to the question 'Do we have enough?' is 'no', you will have to look very hard at the capital tied up in your house. Trading off the home that you have lived in for so long may well be worth it if it means you are able to do the things and live the life you have always wanted. It can be hard, but ultimately you have to decide what is important to you.

At the other end of the spectrum, some people sell up and resolve to rent for the rest of their lives. This can work particularly well for people who have decided to spend a lot of their new life travelling or working overseas.

Many will have to consider how they might access the capital in their house. The house may seem like an unattractive item to trade, but it may be necessary if you really want to live the life you want.

Walk the line

Where you draw the line between the house that you own and your other assets, that is, income-earning investment capital, can make a huge difference to how well you enjoy your twenty good summers. Some people have a lot of house and not much capital to generate income, while others have a more modest house and lot of income from their capital. Ultimately, where you draw this line is up to you and the life that you want to live, but it is something that needs to be thought through.

It is best to explain this by way of an example. Take a couple with a combined net worth of $1.5 million. If they draw the line so that they have $1.2 million of that capital in their house and the remaining $300,000 to generate income, they should certainly have a very nice house. They may enjoy the garden and the swimming pool and regard the time that they have at the house as the best thing that they can do. In addition, they should have approximately $250 per week from their $300,000 income-generating capital—it is not much if they want to do things other than enjoy the swimming pool and work in the garden. On the other hand, they could sell that house and own a unit to the value of $500,000 and invest the remaining $1 million. This should give them an income of over $750 per week—enough to travel and live fairly well, although the house will probably not give them as much pleasure.

You have a choice that effectively comes down to how much house versus how much income you will have. As a rough rule of thumb, each $100,000 that you have in a house could generate $4–5,000 of income. You may want the expensive house as you take a great deal of pleasure from it or you may prefer to travel and do other things. It is up to you to make a conscious decision because only you know what gives you the greatest satisfaction.

12 | Factor four: inheritances

When most people look at whether or not they will 'have enough' to last them the rest of their lives, they look only at the income they can derive from their capital. They neglect the fact that they have capital, and that capital can be spent.

If you think back to the discussion of the chicken farmer living on eggs, you will remember that the chickens were the farmer's capital and the eggs his income. The chicken farmer did not have enough capital chickens to provide him with sufficient income eggs and solved this problem by working for a neighbour and being paid in eggs. This is a reasonable solution, but there are others. One of the other options would be to eat a few chickens, which would no doubt make a very nice change from all those eggs. Changing your diet so that you start to eat some chickens does mean that you can eat more, but it also means that you will have less capital—fewer chickens—and therefore, gradually, a diminishing income—number of eggs. When living off both capital and income, you are effectively in a race to ensure that your money does not run out before you do.

I have often said at seminars and conferences that you can let the cheque to the undertaker bounce; that is, you can go out on the last dollar. Some would go further than this and let the cheques for last week's ski holiday in Switzerland and the wonderful dinner the previous night bounce as well. Spending capital in this way means that you will not be the richest person in the cemetery. Besides, I have never thought that was a worthy goal. If you want to spend all your capital and can get it right, the graph of your net worth will look like this:

Figure 12.1: Spending all your capital in your lifetime

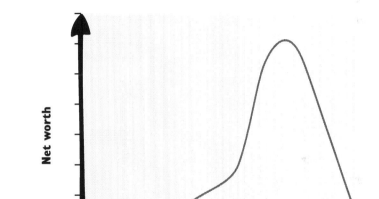

I have considered the idea that you can take your wealth with you when you die, and I have to say that the evidence for this is pretty skinny. You do need to spend it in this world because it is very doubtful that it will be legal tender in the next. However, there are a couple of things that mitigate against spending all your capital and going out on that last dollar:

- Most of us want to leave an inheritance to our children. In spite of what some people say about spending their kids' inheritance, I think that most people do want to leave at least something, and often quite a lot. This is probably hard-wired into us—we want to promote our genetic material and an inheritance does help that.

- Most of us don't know when we are going to die and, therefore, don't know how much longer we have. If we knew exactly how long we had, it would be a very simple exercise with a financial calculator to work out how much of our money—capital and interest—we could spend on a weekly basis. But most of us do not know, and the fear of the money running out before we do is great. There is a way around this—the purchase of an annuity mortgage, as discussed in Chapter 11.

Ultimately, how much of your capital you want to spend and how much you want to leave as an inheritance is a philosophical decision, one that we must all make individually or as a family. The amount of capital you are prepared to spend will affect the amount of inheritance you can leave. Conversely, you can establish the amount you want to leave as inheritances and spend the rest. Some people decide to keep their house mortgage free to eventually go as inheritances to the kids, while they quite happily spend other assets and investments.

The net-worth graph for most people does not show their capital declining very much, certainly not so much that it will go to zero. I do know people who keep growing their net worth so that their graph looks like this:

Figure 12.2: Net worth over a lifetime

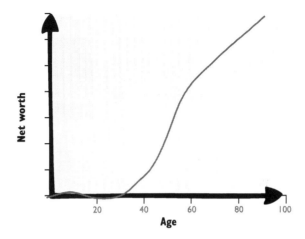

A lot of people would think that continuing to grow net worth was not very sensible. In which case, the graph for net worth may look something like this:

Figure 12.3: Maintaining peak net worth

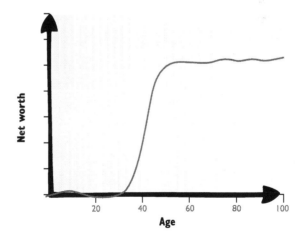

One thing to bear in mind when making this philosophical decision is that by the time you leave your inheritance to your children they are likely to be quite old themselves. If, for example, you had children at the age of thirty and you die at the age of ninety, your children will be sixty when they receive their inheritance. It is likely by that time that they will be well established professionally and financially—we would hope so, anyway! You could argue that it would be better to spend the money early to give your children the benefit of a good education that will help them throughout their lives.

Whatever you decide about inheritances or use of capital will be an important part of your plan for a new life. It is a factor that you can adjust quite well if you find that the answer to the question 'Do we have enough?' is negative. You may decide to spend capital cautiously, so that it does not run out too soon, to make the financial plan work. For example, if you found that your income from investments and part-time work was going to leave you $500 per month in deficit, you could decide to start to supplement your income by spending capital.

Receiving an inheritance

While we are thinking about inheritances and the family issues involved, it is useful to mention here that you may well receive one yourself at some point in the future, which will obviously be added to the amount of capital you already have. Some people regard an inheritance as not really being their own money. Instead, they consider themselves the custodians of this money, investing it and hoping to pass it on to their own children and grandchildren and, so, keep it in the family.

Dealing with an inheritance can be quite a lot more complicated than dealing with money you have saved. The receipt of an inheritance is usually coloured with sadness and sometimes tinged with guilt. It may well be the biggest sum of money you ever receive in your life.

You can never completely rely on receiving an inheritance, however. In trying to answer the question 'Do we have enough?', you may be fairly sure that you will receive an inheritance and you may even have a fairly good idea of how much it is likely to be—but you cannot be certain. Therefore, in answering the question, I would suggest that you do not factor in the receipt of an inheritance unless there is some unusual circumstance that makes it virtually guaranteed. It seems to me that to decide that you are going to have enough to work less and live more because you think you might receive an inheritance is a recipe for trouble.

So, what should you do when you receive an inheritance? The simple answer is nothing—at least, not for a few months anyway. A time of emotional difficulty is not the best time to make investment decisions, particularly when it concerns perhaps the biggest amount of money you have been given to manage. Put the inheritance away in a bank term deposit for a few months while you think about what to do with it.

Ultimately, the money is likely to be added to your other investment funds. Some people will hold inheritance money as custodians for future generations, but most will use it for their own purposes. When an inheritance arrives you can add the amount to your net worth—it may make all the difference to whether or not you have enough to live the life you want in your retirement.

13 | Factor five: how much will you work?

At the age of sixty, I am still not sure what I am going to do when I grow up. At present I am well into my fourth fairly distinct career, and guess that I have at least one career to come. I never intend to give up work, although I recognise that at some point in the future this might change. If I keep doing some kind of paid work for another twenty years or so, you can see that I still have a bit of time to work out what I am going to do when I finally grow up.

Few people want to simply set up a chair in the shade or by the heater and spend their days sitting in it. Similarly, few people want to spend all day every day on the golf course, in the garden, travelling or out fishing. Most of us want some kind of focus to our lives and something to strive and aim for. In fact, for many of us it is critical that we have something to strive for—there is no life if we are not pushing to improve ourselves or other things. If you are in your forties, fifties or sixties, you are much too young to just withdraw from the real world.

Most of the clients I've had for WealthPlanning don't want to retire. They want to work less, they want more time and they want less pressure. But they do not want to buy themselves a rocking chair and sit in it for thirty years waiting to die. They want to work, sometimes for the money and sometimes to give some structure to their lives and usually so that they feel useful. Interestingly, virtually every client that I have ever had has said that when they are financially free, they want to put a lot of their time into charitable or community work.

Having said this, there are of course some people who do not want to work at all, preferring to retire in the traditional sense. These people are going to have to fund their lifestyles to a greater extent from somewhere else, perhaps deciding to leave a smaller inheritance, downsizing the house, working a bit longer so that there is more capital saved, and so on. In answering the question 'Do we have enough?', these people are a bit more likely to get a negative reply. Quite simply, without some income from paid work, there will have to be adjustment of at least one of the other seven factors.

In my experience, for a lot of people the amount they are going to work to earn income is often the last factor to be adjusted. People will look at all the other things they have and want—their lifestyle, the amount of investment return they can get from their capital, the size and cost of the house—and work until there is no deficit. In other words, they will work to the extent needed to make up the gap between what they want to spend and what they will receive from investments and other sources.

This sees people doing all sorts of things, from working as consultants to taking on special assignments, driving taxis, filling in while others are on holiday, making and selling furniture, and doing odd jobs. The bit of money they get from these activities makes all the difference to their lifestyles.

Others work because they really want to, so that they are out in society, meeting people and making a difference.

Redundancy

I have seen many people have their lives disrupted by enforced redundancy close to retirement. It is all very well for someone like me to encourage people to keep working, but when you lose your job in your fifties or sixties it can be very difficult to find another. People have reported to me that even a quite low-paying job can be hard to find as employers are thinking that an older person will not fit in with all of the other staff they have in their teens or twenties.

There is not much really that you can do about this except to be aware of it and try to keep your network fresh and your skills honed. Redundancy or business failure can throw you into the job market at any time, regardless of how good your current position in a firm. It pays to be thinking of plan B.

Professional people often carry on working part time; for example, lawyers become consultants to their firms, working a day or two a week; engineers take on occasional assignments; accountants keep doing the books for a few favourite clients; managers take on locums, stepping in to let the usual manager take extended leave; and people with all sorts of skills become consultants taking on occasional clients.

Of course, there are also people who work partly because they want to and partly because they have to. People who can choose whether or not they work at all are the lucky ones.

However, if you have to work to make the pieces of the plan fit, you can take some comfort from knowing that even if you did have the choice, you would probably choose to be in some sort of paid employment.

While most people want to work for many years after they have eased back, you have to be fairly careful when establishing a plan that relies on a certain amount of income. This whole area of work is difficult to plan with any precision because of three things:

- You could change your mind—it is easy enough to say, at the age of fifty, that you will always want to keep up with some sort of work. The road to hell can be paved with the best of intentions and things might look a bit different later on. Although your intention might be to work for another twenty-five years, things may not seem so much fun later on. You cannot therefore be certain that you will have some income from work for all of that time.

- The type of work you do is important. Many countries now have laws that mean you cannot be fired because of your age. Nevertheless, some jobs are better suited than others to people who are getting on a bit. If you are an accountant, for example, you can happily carry on adding up figures for as long as you can sit upright, nearly! If you are a builder, however, you probably don't want to be crawling around on the roof of a two-storey house attaching tiles and you will want to find something else to work at, which will take a bit of planning as you may have to re-skill or up-skill. Finding another occupation that fits your skills, in part at least, and adding new skills and getting some experience is not that hard to organise, provided you give yourself a bit of lead time.

- You could get ill or be injured. Health problems can derail plans at any age, and that includes people who have decided to ease back a bit. If you are dependent on the money that you are planning to earn from work, you could find yourself in difficulty if you have not insured against this happening.

These three things mean that you do not really know how long you will be able to work. You can take an educated guess, but that guess is likely to be a lot more accurate in the short term than it will be in the longer term. Nevertheless, it is reasonable to assume that you will be able to earn some income from work for a considerable time, and I think your plans should include it. Just be aware that bad things can happen and derail your plans but, of course, that can happen to anyone at any time. Most of the clients I have worked with have planned to continue to work indefinitely and have planned to use the income that they receive from it.

Part-time options

There are nearly always options for people who are looking for part-time work. While the work you find may not be exactly what you were doing before, there are usually ways you can apply your skills for best reward.

A real estate agent could consider:

- Office work for other real estate agents
- Sales training

- Preparing houses for sale
- Other sales areas.

A manager could consider:

- Consultancy
- Locum contracts
- Directorships
- Mentoring
- Part ownership of a small business—with a director's/consultant's role.

A teacher could consider:

- After-school child care
- Commission sales
- Tutoring/coaching
- Relieving
- Care for children in holidays
- Adult education in areas of outside interest/expertise.

A business owner could consider:

- Part ownership
- Consultancy
- Locum contracts
- Tutoring
- Staff training
- Troubleshooting
- Directorships.

Most people have work skills that cross over into other professions. You may have to think about the skills you have and take some advice, but it is likely that you will find something you can enjoy and gives you income.

14 | Factor six: other income

Many people have income from sources other than work, investments or a business. This other income obviously has to be taken into account when you are trying to answer the question 'Do we have enough?' Not only do you have to identify what other income you have, but you should also look to maximise those income streams and look for new ones.

The types of things that people have as other income are:

• Superannuation payments
• Government assistance
• Payments from family members
• Taking in a boarder
• Income from a family trust
• Payments from family trusts and estates
• Annuities
• Payments from family businesses
• Royalty payments
• Renting the house while travelling.

These items of income can be quite important. In some cases they may be quite large and form a significant part of the income you are going to have. This list is almost certainly not exhaustive—people have all sorts of circumstances, and it never ceases to surprise me what people have as income from quite unusual sources.

One area where I do see potential income for clients is from their children. This may sound a bit harsh on first reading, and I really am not advocating sending them out to work solely to keep you in laid-back bliss, although perhaps I should be—maybe there is a use for children after all. The area where I see children being a problem with respect to other income is when they return home at the end of an overseas trip or at the end of a relationship—and stay! This is surprisingly common these days as children in their twenties and thirties often behave like boomerangs.

Well, of course it is nice to have them, but in my experience they simply move back into their old room that, along with the contents of the fridge, they regard as their own property. In this case, I think it is very reasonable to ask them for board or, at the very least, a contribution to household costs. If the board they pay is anything near market levels the amount can be calculated as 'other income'. The only problem with budgeting in this other income is that it is unlikely to last forever—you can be fairly sure that they will be off overseas again or into another relationship soon enough. It is unlikely that when you are in your eighties and your eldest son is in his fifties he will still be living with you. The income from him is unlikely to be dependable. Nevertheless, you could commit yourselves to always having a boarder or two, whether these boarders are your children or other people.

Decisions about the category 'other income' are a very individual thing. It can come from a range of sources and, in a few cases, could be increased with a bit of thought. You do, however, need to consider how secure it is and how long it is likely to last. Nevertheless, as one of the eight factors making up the answer to the question 'Do we have enough?', it does need to be considered and accounted for.

15 | Factor seven: life expectancy

Strictly speaking, your age is not really a factor in how much you will need. Calling this chapter 'Life expectancy' is really only a polite way of asking when you think you are going to die. This chapter is really about how long you have left to live; that is, how long is your money going to have to last? The fear we all have is that the money will run out before we do—it seems therefore to be fairly useful, when asking if you will have enough, to think about the length of time your money has to last. This clearly is a factor that, for most, cannot be calculated with any precision at all. It is also a factor which really only concerns people who are going to spend some or all of their capital.

On the other hand, if you are intending to keep your capital intact to be passed on to the next generation while you live solely on the investment returns, it is not a factor you need to bother with although, even then, you need to be aware of the effects of inflation, as discussed in Chapter 16. In this case, the only real question is whether you are going to pass on the amount of your capital in real terms or nominal terms. The difference between the two is simply inflation. If you have $200,000 of savings and you want to pass this on to your children when you die in, say, thirty years, the spending power of that $200,000 will be much less than it is today. Even the current relatively low inflation rate whittles away at the value of capital and income if you do not regularly increase that capital by 2–3 per cent per annum.

However, even those who want to pass on their capital intact to the next generation need to think about living off their capital or, more accurately, living off their capital gains. This is because you will need to invest in things other than just bank deposits and bonds. You will want to invest in growth assets like shares and property, because over long periods of time these give better total returns, in that they give income, income growth and capital gains. You need to be able to live off the income from your investments, but you will probably have to draw on the capital gain as well. If you do not draw on the capital you will probably continue to get richer, which in many cases is not what you want. You have probably spent the last thirty years or so building up your wealth and savings, but now that you are going to ease back there seems little point continuing to do so. You will want to be able to draw on the total return from your investments, which means accessing the capital growth that you have.

If you are going to use some of your capital to live on, you do need to think about how long it will last. As noted previously, you are unlikely to be able to do this with any degree of accuracy—few of us know when we are going to die. In my experience, people considering this factor very wisely behave conservatively; that is, they add a few more years to the number of years over which they are planning to use their capital. The perfect financial plan may be to see the cheque to the undertaker bounce, but in practice this is not as easy as it sounds. Clearly, it is better to overestimate the amount of time you need your capital to last than to underestimate it and find yourself living your last few years in penury.

Estimating the number of years you are likely to live is part science, part guesswork. Some of the things to consider are:

- Life expectancy figures—remember that life expectancy rises as people get older, so that a thirty-year-old might have a life expectancy of seventy-eight years, but the same person at the age of sixty-five could have a life expectancy of eighty-five years. Remember, also, that life expectancy figures are very broad, giving averages across total populations. The variance between individuals is huge.
- Life expectancy is rising—better healthcare means that we should live longer and better and some experts say that a person born in 2000 has a 50 per cent chance of living to one hundred.
- Family history—although this is no guarantee that you will not be run over by a bus tomorrow, longevity runs in some families, so family history does give some pointers.
- General health and fitness is fairly subjective, but in many cases it may be the biggest factor, whether on the upside or the downside.

You can look at these things quite carefully, but you are still going to have to make a guess. I have thought that I might make ninety—I have a good family history in this regard and keep myself fairly fit, but if I were going to spend capital I would plan for longer than that. Nevertheless, the worst could happen at any time—I could have a major health problem tomorrow, or fall off a mountain next week although my early death would most likely be caused by Joan carrying out her threat to kill me if I leave the toilet seat up one more time.

The practicalities of living off capital can be problematic. Not only do you not know how long it will need to last, but you also have to have your investments arranged so you can draw capital as you need it. This of course is no problem if your investments are bank deposits—you can draw on your savings at will. But many of us are expecting to be living off capital for a long period, and having all our savings in bank deposits is not the best way to invest. The length of time you will be investing—almost certainly decades—means that you really should have a lot of your money in growth assets, such as shares and property. If you are going to be investing for twenty or thirty summers, or even longer, you do need to be in better-performing, albeit more risky and volatile, assets like shares and property.

Your age and, therefore, how long your money is likely to have to last are the most difficult and unknowable of all the eight factors. It is also one of the most important—get the answer seriously wrong and your money could run out well before you do, and you could, for many years, have a significantly poorer lifestyle than you were hoping for. It can have a big influence on the answer to the question 'How much will we need?', particularly when you are considering whether or not you will spend capital.

16 | Factor eight: the returns you will get

Conventional wisdom says that on retirement you should sell your growth assets—property and shares—and invest in things like bank deposits, company debentures and bonds. These things are deemed to be the safest forms of investments to give the income that you need, which is true.

However, what is also true is that you are not retiring in the conventional sense. You are easing back to enjoy twenty good summers and, possibly, quite a few more than that. You need to be able to use your capital for income for some decades, which is a long time-frame in investment terms. The problem you face is that even our current, reasonably benign rate of inflation will, over those decades, erode your spending power. Furthermore, you probably need higher returns than those offered by bank deposits, company debentures and bonds, and given the time-frame you can afford to seek them.

I think that conventional wisdom should, therefore, be discarded. True enough, you do need to invest reasonably securely and you do want income, but debt-type investments, such as bank deposits, debentures and bonds, are not the only options. In fact, I think that a significant proportion of your investment portfolio should be in ownership assets that will grow; that is, shares and property. This is because, although these things may carry more risk and show more volatility, they do provide both capital growth and income growth. This growth is critical if you are to get good returns and maintain the spending power of your capital and income.

The secret, then, is to invest some of your money in higher-return assets while trying to keep risk as low as possible. You do not do this by answering advertisements in the newspaper and investing in third- or fourth-rate finance companies that offer, say, 11 or 12 per cent. In fact, you do not do it by going only into debt investments. You do it by diversifying, with a good proportion of what you own remaining in shares and property.

In a nutshell, the returns from top-class debt investments that only give income, such as bank deposits and government bonds, are likely to be too low, while third- and fourth-rate finance companies are too risky. That leaves ownership investments—shares and property. These will give the returns that you want but they will show some volatility, so you have to realise that the possibility of complete failure of any one company is higher.

There are four things you can do to reduce the risks of ownership investments:

- Diversify—I am not suggesting that all your investment funds should be in ownership investments. You should have some bonds and bank deposits, investments that will undoubtedly lower your returns, but also smooth out the volatility, reduce absolute risk and give you some ready money when economic times are tough.
- Choose quality shares and quality property. In the case of company shares it means companies with good, safe cash

flows. Utility companies and those with very strong brands with high barriers to entry fit this category. In the case of property, this means reasonably new buildings with good long-term leases in good locations.

- Have no debt, or very little.
- Have a fairly high proportion of cash to act as a buffer, as discussed in Chapter 20.

In trying to calculate how much you will need, the returns you are likely to get can be one of the hardest things to decide. This is partly because you have to look at how much risk you can take, but it is also because you are likely to be relying, to some extent at least, on your investments for a long period of time. Over those years and decades there are likely to be many ups and downs with economic boom times, economic stagnation and economic meltdowns. You are in the position of not wanting a major loss that will force you back to work full time.

If you are risk averse, you should go more into good-quality debt investments. This will lower your returns, but if it lets you sleep better so be it. The benchmark of investment returns of 8 per cent is for people who are prepared to tolerate volatility. If you cannot accept some volatility, you have to accept lower returns. Furthermore, do take some advice from a professional adviser—someone who will assess your risk profile and will suggest investment options that suit your particular circumstances.

My benchmark for returns from Security Assets is that you should be able to get a return of 8 per cent before tax. I acknowledge that this is hard at the moment although, even now, it is by no means impossible. It is hard simply because interest rates are low and share and property values are high, meaning that cash yields are low. This will not last forever—there will be times when interest rates and property and share yields are more attractive. You may have to be patient! Nevertheless, depending on a range of factors, including your appetite for risk, the duration that you choose to invest for, your investment skill, and whether you invest directly or through managed funds, you should be able to get an investment return of somewhere in the range of 8 per cent before tax on your Security Assets.

Inflation

You also need to think about that old bogey, inflation. The yield you are getting on your investments might be enough to live on in today's dollar terms, but even a low inflation rate of, say, 2 per cent will erode the value of your investment over time. You need to think about this. While an 8 per cent yield may give you enough at the moment, if it does not grow it will not be enough later, unless you can tolerate a lower standard of living. You also need to watch out for inflation because if it gets away again, as it did in the 1970s and 1980s, you could be in serious trouble. Inflation is very bad for people on fixed incomes; that is, people who only have debt investments where there is no prospect of income growth.

All the calculations you do to work out if you have enough, and the examples in Chapter 17, are based on what income you will have in the first year of easing back. In, say, twenty years, you may have the same nominal income but it will not have the same spending power.

There are four things to consider when planning to take account of inflation:

- Remember that your expenditure is likely to decrease as you get older. Expenditure will not fall in a straight line, but it is likely that your expenditure at the age of eighty will be lower than at sixty-five.
- Invest at least some of your money in growth investments. It must already be apparent that I believe this is what most people should do. Property and shares should both show capital and income growth over long periods of time.
- Decide that you will make up for the effects of inflation by using a part or all of your capital to supplement your income. This will necessarily mean smaller inheritances to the kids.
- Reinvest. Even if your investment portfolio is going to yield 8 per cent per annum, plan in the early years to spend only a part of this income so that your wealth is growing a little at the beginning. Over time, you slowly start to spend more and more of your income. For example, if you are getting 8 per cent per annum on your investments, plan to only use 6 per cent in the early years, reinvesting the remaining 2 per cent for the future.

Incorporating inflation into your calculations is very difficult because of two factors:

- We do not know what the rate of inflation is likely to be over the next twenty or thirty years. We can hope that it will be around 2 per cent, but it could be more and it could be less. It may even be that we have a period of deflation, which would pose a whole new set of problems.
- We do not know how long we are going to live. We can take an educated guess at it and allow a few more years to

ensure we come out on the right side of the equation, but it is possible that inflation could eat away at your capital and income for forty years or more.

Although you may never be able to calculate the precise effects of inflation on your capital and income, you need to allow for it in your long-term planning. In my view, this means being fairly careful and cautious, making sure when you answer the question 'Do we have enough?' that your income does more than simply match your expenditure for the next year. A tight budget like that will inevitably lead to problems in the future—it will mean that, although you could answer, 'yes, we have enough' in the early years, you could find in a few years' time that your answer will be, 'no, now we don't have enough'. Be conservative in your plans and make sure that you have a good part of your investment portfolio in growth assets.

In summary, to plan how you are going to live when you are earning less from work, you need to think about the returns that you will get from your investment capital. With a diversified portfolio, my benchmark of 8 per cent before tax is quite possible over a lengthy period, but there will be some ups and downs. A return of this magnitude before tax translates to perhaps 5 per cent after tax. If you are more risk averse you may aim for a somewhat lower return than this, using more investments like bank deposits and government bonds.

17 | So, do you have enough?

To answer the question posed by this chapter title, you will have to work your way through each of the eight factors discussed in chapters 9 to 16. These factors are:

- The amount of capital you have
- The lifestyle you want
- The house you want
- Inheritances
- How much you will work
- Other income
- Life expectancy
- The returns you will get.

Unfortunately, you cannot do this entirely by numbers. Answering this question, like some of the others, is part science, part art. There is a good bit of judgment involved, as well as prediction of the future. However, there is a template, on page 109, that asks the right questions and lets you fill in some numbers to see if you will have enough. The process is not meant to be exact but is enough to give you a reasonable indication. It is the one I use in WealthCoaching to calculate the Freedom Figure for clients.

The calculation process is iterative. You have to look at each item, seeing if you can live happily on what you have. If the answer is 'no', you have to adjust and re-do the plan, and keep on re-doing it until you are satisfied you have enough. If the answer continues to be 'no', then you probably don't have enough yet and had better keep working and growing your wealth. Even if the final answer is 'no', the process will at least allow you to see what your Freedom Figure is, and thus give you a goal to work towards.

Freedom Figure calculation

Step 1
Calculate your net worth (see page 66). Include your house in this exercise.

Step 2
Deduct the value of the house you want to live in when you have eased back. This may be of less value than the one you now live in if you are planning to downsize.

Step 3
Deduct the value of any major lifestyle assets that you plan to buy (holiday house, boat, etc.).

Step 4
Having deducted steps 2 and 3 from Step 1, you now have the amount of capital available to invest.

Step 5
Apply the before-tax return you are likely to get from your investments. Allow for inflation, especially if investing mainly in debt investments.

Step 6

Add any income you expect to receive from ongoing work.

Step 7

Add any other income you are likely to receive (e.g. superannuation, annuities, taking in a boarder).

Step 8

This is your total income before tax. Now deduct tax to get an after-tax figure.

Step 9

Do an expenditure budget and enter the figure for living costs here.

Step 10

Deduct Step 9 from Step 8. This is your surplus or deficit.

If you have a surplus

Congratulations! You have enough to ease back and enjoy a lot of really good summers.

If you have a deficit

Don't give up yet! You need to go back to the beginning and run through the assumptions you have made, and do the numbers again. If the deficit is not too great, you may still have options. Ask yourself:

- Are you sure that your net-worth statement is correct?
- Can you downsize the house?
- Do you really need those lifestyle assets (boat, etc.)?

- Can you get higher returns?
- Are you prepared to live off capital to some extent?
- Can you cut the expenditure for your lifestyle?
- Are you sure that you can have no other income?

If you still have a deficit

You are probably going to have to work longer and continue to build up your capital. Work through the process again to see how much capital would make things work and allow you to ease back.

If you still don't have enough:

- Work out how much you will need (your Freedom Figure).
- Put a time to when you will achieve this.
- Write down your Freedom Figure and the time by which you will achieve it—this is your big financial goal.
- Plan to use the time that you have to retrain so that you can continue to work part time.

It may be that you come back again to this process when you have finished this book.

Example I

Tom and Jenny are ready to semi-retire. They are both teachers, living in a large city, but are planning to move to a smaller town to be nearer their children (and impending grandchild).

Freedom Figure calculation

Step 1

Calculate your net worth (see page 66). Include your house in this exercise.

Tom and Jenny have a net worth of $950 000. They have a house worth $700,000 and investments of $250,000.

Step 2

Deduct the value of the house you want to live in when you have eased back. This may be of less value than the one you now live in if you are planning to downsize.

Tom and Jenny are moving to the country and so would downsize the house to one worth $500,000.

Step 3

Deduct the value of any major lifestyle assets that you plan to buy (holiday house, boat, etc.).

Tom and Jenny plan to do a lot of travelling in a motor home and have budgeted $50,000 to buy this and a boat.

Step 4

Having deducted steps 2 and 3 from Step 1, you now have the amount of capital available to invest.

$400,000 to invest (total net worth of $950,000 less $500,000 for the house and less $50,000 for the motor home and boat).

Step 5

Apply the before-tax return you are likely to get from your investments.

Tom and Jenny aim to achieve a return of 8 per cent before tax ($400,000 @ 8% = $32,000).

Step 6
Add any income you expect to receive from ongoing work.
Tom and Jenny are both going to coach maths and reading and expect to earn a total of $20,000 p.a. between them.

Step 7
Add any other income you are likely to receive (e.g. superannuation, annuities, taking in a boarder).
None.

Step 8
This is your total income before tax.
Investment income: $32,000
Coaching income: $20,000
Now deduct tax to get an after-tax figure.
After-tax income: $40,000

Step 9
Do an expenditure budget and enter the figure for living costs here.
Living costs: $35,000

Step 10
Deduct Step 9 from Step 8. This is your surplus or deficit.
Surplus: $5,000 (This may be added back to capital to keep up with inflation.)

Tom and Jenny can start to plan for their new life with some confidence. There is not a great surplus but enough (and they know that if they have to they can go back to teaching, unattractive though that idea may be). The $5,000 surplus can be reinvested for a few years, which will help cover them for inflation.

Example 2

Clint owns an auto-electrical business. The business has three staff (the management of whom provides a constant head-ache for Clint). He is sick of his business and at fifty-one wants to travel (something he missed out on when he was younger).

Freedom Figure calculation

Step 1
Calculate your net worth (see page 66). Include your house in this exercise.
Clint has a net worth of $740,000 (his house at $500,000 and the business worth $240,000).

Step 2
Deduct the value of the house you want to live in when you have eased back. This may be of less value than the one you now live in if you are planning to downsize.
Clint wants to continue to live in his house.

Step 3
Deduct the value of any major lifestyle assets that you plan to buy (holiday house, boat, etc.).
None.

Step 4

Having deducted steps 2 and 3 from Step 1, you now have the amount of capital available to invest.

Clint will have $240,000 to invest provided that he can sell the business.

Step 5

Apply the before-tax return you are likely to get from your investments.

Clint knows nothing about investment but a financial adviser tells him that he should get 8 per cent before tax.

Step 6

Add any income you expect to receive from ongoing work.

Clint has an opportunity to teach his trade at the local technical college and should earn around $10,000 p.a.

Step 7

Add any other income you are likely to receive (e.g. superannuation, annuities, taking in a boarder).

None.

Step 8

This is your total income before tax.

Investment income: $19,200 ($240,000 @ 8% = $19,200)

Teaching income: $10,000

Total before-tax income: $29,200

Now deduct tax to get an after-tax figure.

After-tax income: $25,000

Step 9

Do an expenditure budget and enter the figure for living costs here.

Living costs: $37,000

Step 10

Deduct Step 9 from Step 8. This is your surplus or deficit.

Deficit: $12,000

Clint is not in a position to sell up and go to a new life yet. He needs to:

- Check to make sure that the business is really worth $240,000 (maybe it is worth more).
- Decide if he really wants to keep the house. Perhaps he could downsize?
- Perhaps look for higher investment returns (although they would have to be very high to close the deficit).
- Consider his budget. Perhaps he can live on less?
- Work more at teaching, perhaps?

Clint is not likely to be able to make the break at this time unless he does something radical like downsizing the house or making a dramatic cut in his budgeted expenditure. Clint needs $12,000 more income p.a. and to get that will need $200,000 more capital invested at 8 per cent before tax to bridge the gap. Even then, Clint will have no buffer if things go wrong, nor would he be allowing for inflation.

My advice to Clint will be to set a goal to achieve an additional net worth of $250,000 in the next three years. He could do this by running the business hard, developing it to make it more saleable at a better price and by taking out profits and saving them. Clint should also be starting to do some tutoring, developing a network at the college so he can get more work than he has been offered. If Clint does these things and does them well, he has a good chance of being able to get out of the business. If he doesn't he could be stuck there, unable to get out until he is able to draw on his superannuation.

Section | 3

Making it work

18 | Arrange (and maximise) your investments

When you start to ease back and earn less your investment strategy will have to change, from a strategy designed to build your wealth to one where you start to live off your wealth. This means moving from having predominantly Wealth-Creating Assets to Security Assets.

This change does not necessarily have to happen suddenly—it may be gradual and progressive over several years. It may take some years simply because you want to pick a good time—when the prices are high—to sell out of some investments and a good time—when the price is right—to buy into others. You should aim for an investment return from your Security Assets of 7–9 per cent before tax. This is lower than what a lot of people aim for when they are younger and are engaged in building up their wealth. Nevertheless, this is still quite a high rate of return before tax—not something you will get by simply putting your money into bank deposits or government bonds.

Your investment needs will have changed. Specifically, you will have to do two things:

- Use your investments for income on which to live, or at least maintain a level of liquidity.
- Lower the amount of risk you take.

There is one big issue that makes the difference between Wealth-Creating Assets and Security Assets—something that both lowers risk and gives you more income. That is the amount of debt you have. Borrowing to own investments is beneficial if you want to build up your wealth quickly, and as such is the key to Wealth-Creating Assets. Borrowing to buy investments—called gearing or leverage—can turn an ordinary investment performance into a stellar investment performance. Gearing up investments will also convert income into capital growth. The cost of borrowing—interest—has to be met, usually out of the rents or dividends from the investment. This means that when you are borrowing to own investments the income you get from them is reduced. However, because you are borrowing to own an investment, you can buy more of an appreciating investment and, so, capital growth will be greater. Gearing therefore means that your income is less, but your capital gains are greater.

Gearing works very well when you are trying to build up your wealth. You do not really want income because, hopefully, you are getting plenty of that from your work or your business. However, when you start to earn less from your job or business and begin to live off your investments, the income you get from your investments is important and reducing cost is critical, the capital growth less so. Gearing works brilliantly for younger people, but when you start to live off the wealth that you have created it is time to look for more income with less risk. This precludes gearing.

The obvious outcome is that you should have much less debt or, preferably, you will be debt free when you ease back. Not only do you want more income and less capital growth, you also need less risk. Gearing works very well when assets are appreciating, but it is a disaster when they fall in value. You can gear up your investments but you can also gear them down as well.

Income and growth

When people ease back and work less or stop work altogether they look for income from their investment portfolios. After all, they no longer want to grow their wealth and it is cash that they have to use to buy groceries. However, this quest for income can make people make some strange and unhelpful investment decisions. Some people take up investments that they would never otherwise consider, and ignore others that they should take up.

The pursuit of income in the past decade, when it has been hard to get a good yield, has seen people invest in things like collateralised debt obligations (CDOs) based on sub-prime mortgages or into third-rate finance company debentures to their cost.

Many investors who are using their investment capital to get income shun growth investments like shares or some unit trusts because of the lack of income. And yet, for me a dollar that has come from capital growth is every bit as good as a dollar that has come from interest or a dividend. In fact, it's better because capital gains are usually taxed more benignly.

After all, if you get some capital growth from shares of trusts you can always sell a few units periodically to take out your capital gain in cash. You do not necessarily need to sell all of your shares or units. You can sell just enough to take out some cash on which to live.

The other thing to be aware of with growth investments is that they do not just give capital growth but, all going well, there is income growth, too. This is important. If you invest only in cash and bonds, your income will decrease in value over the years as inflation does its destructive work. Therefore, having some of your portfolio in growth investments is important to all long-term investors.

When you choose to earn less you should sell some of your investments and repay debt, thus removing interest costs. It might mean that you sell some of your investment property, repaying the mortgages you have on them, and use the equity to retire other mortgages. It might mean selling off investments to repay the house mortgage. It might mean cashing up any shares or investment warrants that have borrowings on them. Again, this does not have to be done in a hurry—you do not have to do it the day you leave your job. Indeed, there could be significant financial disadvantages to doing this in a hurry; for example, if you have a fixed-rate mortgage you will want to wait until the fixed period has expired. If the market is in a down period, you would not sell into the gloom just because that is the day you are leaving your job and moving to the country. You do want to get yourself into a position of being debt free, but it does not have to be immediate.

The difference between a Wealth-Creating Asset and a Security Asset is often gearing; that is, the level of associated debt. For example, a property with 80 per cent of its value borrowed is certainly a Wealth-Creating Asset—it is quite risky but likely to show very high returns over time. The same property with no debt is a Security Asset—it is quite safe, but will give good income with some moderate growth as well.

Risk and return can also be about the degree to which you have diversified—a share portfolio with only four or five elements means that the investor is taking a big position; a share portfolio spread across many industries and several different countries will perhaps show lower returns but will definitely be less volatile.

The transition to Security Assets should not be difficult, even though it may take some time to complete. You have to get yourself into a position where you are well diversified with quality income-producing assets with little or no borrowings. This will probably mean that you have to sell some of the investments you currently own to retire debt and invest in other, safer investments. The things that you sell will be things like your business, if you have one, highly geared property and some shares, particularly if you have a lot of just one company.

The investments suitable as Security Assets are:

- Diversified shares
- Property with no or low borrowings
- Bank deposits
- Cash-management trust
- Good-quality bonds
- Managed funds based on any of the above
- Good-quality finance-company deposits

- Good-quality debenture stock
- Capital-guaranteed hedge funds
- Diversified managed funds.

These are the sorts of things you should be aiming to transfer your wealth into. They are not very exciting, but then excitement is not really the point. You want your money working quietly away for you, producing returns without too much worry. While you may prefer to be quite active in the management of your investments, you do not want everything hanging on the performance of a particular market or investment. That means setting things up so that you can get on and enjoy the next however many summers you have left.

The transition

I have already said that you do not need to make the transition from Wealth-Creating Assets to Security Assets in a big hurry. In fact, there is every reason why you should not do so. Just because 25 October is the day you leave your job and start to work as a consultant, or the day you sell your business, does not make it the perfect day for either selling investments or buying them. This is really about trying to time the market, something that, while difficult, is not impossible to do. The small ups and downs of markets are very difficult to predict, but the bigger movements are easier. It is possible to look at the returns you might get from a particular investment market and judge that they are not high enough to make an investment because that market has just had a major run-up. In that situation you would choose to wait until the market has come back to a more realistic level, which could take several years. In the meantime, you would be best to hold cash and wait. Holding cash may seem frustrating, but it seems to me better to do this than to invest at a time that is really not good. Conversely, you may judge that a particular time is not good to sell into and then you would wait until the market improves before cashing up.

Patience is a great virtue in this respect. Because you are playing with your life's savings, you are much better off missing an opportunity than being stampeded into doing something hasty. There is an old investment saying: 'Buy in gloom, sell in boom'. It is much harder to do it than it is to write it, but following this advice, which means taking a contrary view to the rest of the market, is very rewarding.

Some people are not concerned with trying to time the market. They follow a strategy called 'dollar–cost averaging'. Dollar–cost averaging means that you buy into a market over a period of time, often some years. Its basic premise is that you are not trying to pick good times to buy. Instead, you drip-feed money into the market on a regular basis—say, monthly or quarterly—and so get an average price over that period. Dollar–cost averaging also works very well when selling. Although some asset types are not good subjects for this approach—for example, your business or a property investment—others, particularly shares, are very good for it. You decide that you are going to transition out of certain shares to go into others, perhaps switching from growth shares to high-dividend shares. If you didn't have a view on whether or not it was a good time to sell, you could sell portions of your shares at regular intervals, and so get an average price for them over that period.

I think dollar–cost averaging is a very good idea for those who are making the transition from Wealth-Creating Assets to Security Assets. It does require patience and it does take some discipline to keep doing it whether the market is up or down. However, dollar–cost averaging will save you from getting caught by a large swing on the downside with a resultant loss. This is your life's savings we're talking about—a major mistake could see you back at work, or back into business, with all your dreams of a better life gone. This is a time to invest cautiously and conservatively, and have a lot of patience. You are better to put the transition to a new life off for a year or two rather than attempt to rearrange your affairs immediately.

The big wait

When markets are booming, everyone wants to be in. But when markets are high, yields are low—that is, the income returns you are likely to get are quite small compared to what you get in more normal times. Investing into a booming market is not only likely to give you lower returns, but it could also lead to a significant loss.

When you are living off your capital, you are dependent on that capital. This means that you have to be even more careful and conservative with it than in the past. While you do want to get a good return, I think you should always err on the side of caution. That may mean waiting, and waiting some more, if that's what's needed.

The thing I find the hardest when markets are booming is stopping people going into them. Many, many times I have had clients who have been cashed up, perhaps because they have sold their business, received an inheritance, got a severance payment or downsized the house. They are looking for good investments. When markets are high there may not be much in the way of good investments, but these people are impatient. They know they can do better than having their money in the bank and they want to do better, now!

Well, it is true that over a long period you can do better than having your money in the bank. But there are times when markets are so highly valued that you are better off with your money in the bank, getting a paltry 6 per cent or so, but at least keeping your money intact so that it is available for investment when markets return to a better level. When dividend yields and property yields are at 1 or 2 per cent you are better to wait than to be sucked into the crowd.

It may seem like a long wait. However, we are talking about your life savings—if in doubt, stay out.

19 | Build a portfolio

Investment is all about balancing risk and return. As someone dependent on the income from capital and needing to protect that capital, you need to set the amount of risk that you are prepared to tolerate. You cannot completely eliminate investment risk—even governments have been known to renege on their bonds at times—but you can significantly reduce it. At the same time you probably cannot afford to accept very low returns, say, the interest on bank deposits. While these are very low risk they will not usually provide sufficient returns for most people to live decently unless they have a large amount invested. You need therefore to find a balance between risk and return—a balance that is right for you.

Aiming to achieve an investment return of 7–9 per cent before tax will almost certainly mean having some ownership investments. If you are not prepared to keep or take on some ownership investments, you will almost certainly have to lower the return target you are aiming for. Accepting lower returns by weighting your portfolio towards good-quality debt investment is a very reasonable thing to do if you cannot tolerate the greater risk that comes with ownership assets.

The main risk that most investors face is volatility risk. Volatility is the amount of thrashing around, the ups and downs of an investment, as demonstrated by the figure below.

Figure 19.1: Volatility risk in investment

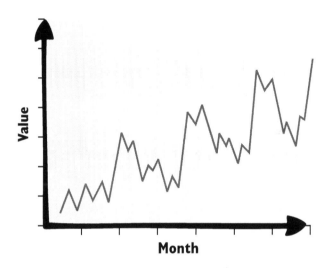

An investment that shows a lot of volatility is likely to give the best returns, but achieving those higher returns could put a strain on your heart as the market thrashes around—it is in downtimes that you are most likely to require the services of a cardiologist. However, we do know it is demonstrable that over the years an asset class, say shares, that goes down a lot will also go up a lot, and over a long period will show better returns than less volatile investments. What you have to think about is how well your heart will stand up to losses, even when they are temporary. Above all, you have to think about how often you can manage a year or two of negative returns. It is possible to model a particular portfolio and say that this group of investments is likely to show losses in one year in every five, while another group is likely to show negative returns one year in every nine. Given that you are investing over a few decades, you need to remember that there will inevitably be some difficult years during that period. You need to think about the level of ups and downs that you can live with, remembering that the higher the returns you seek, the more volatility you will have to withstand.

Debt investments, such as bank deposits and bonds, are likely to show less volatility than ownership investments, such as shares and property. Moreover, all else being equal, debt investments are less likely to show absolute losses; that is, they are less likely to crash and burn. In the case of a company's liquidation, the people who have lent the company money have priority for repayment over the people who own the company. Volatility is one thing, but complete investment failure is another! Although, when all else is equal, there is a greater chance of complete failure from ownership investments than debt investments, all else is seldom equal. There is certainly a greater chance of the complete failure of a third- or fourth-tier finance company taking down both its debt investors and its ownership investors than there is of the complete failure of a solid industrial or utility company.

Debt investments have an important place in building a portfolio. Their place is to give you cash that will always be there regardless of the state of the markets. Holding cash means that, during one of the downtimes you will periodically face, you will not have to sell shares or property. Being a forced seller into a bad market is one of the biggest causes of investment loss. Holding some bank deposits means you can use these to live on if you need to, while you ride out the negative times of a volatile market. This is a very good way of dealing with market volatility.

Investor type

The first and most important thing to do, before you develop an investment strategy, is to identify what type of investor you are. There are five to choose from:

- Defensive
- Conservative
- Balanced
- Growth
- Aggressive.

There are online questionnaires to help you work out where you fit, but there are two questions that largely determine investor type:

- How long you are planning to invest for? A thirty year old will be looking at a much longer time-frame than someone about to start enjoying twenty good summers.
- What is your appetite for risk? For example, a nervous, worrying type is likely to get rattled out of the market, as discussed in the box on page 161.

Your investor type will determine your asset allocation; that is, the proportion of your funds that will go to each of the main asset classes of shares, property, bonds and cash. Obviously, aggressive, growth-seeking investors are people with a greater appetite for risk. This means they are likely to have a greater allocation to shares and property. Defensive and conservative investors are likely to have a greater allocation to cash and bonds. A lot of shares and property in a portfolio will give better returns over long periods of time, but a great deal of volatility along the way. A portfolio with more cash and bonds will be steadier but will show poorer returns in the longer term.

Research shows that it is asset allocation that is the prime determinant of investment performance—the returns you get are related to the volatility you experience in the getting. Achieving the right balance will mean a happy fit between you and your investments. Getting it wrong could be a disaster with returns that are too low or more volatility than you can stand.

The key to worry-free investment is diversification. To build wealth you want just one asset—a business, shares or property—that you drive hard to make yourself as wealthy as possible. As you become dependent on your savings, you want many more investment types giving strength and security to what you own. Note that it does not matter how much investment capital you have—diversification is still the key. Whether you have $50,000 or $5 million to invest, the rules are the same. Someone with a lot of money may be able to carry a bit more risk, but they will still want to avoid having all their money in just one or two investments. As we get older, none of us want to take risks that we could not recover from. The way to cut risk is to retire debt and to diversify.

You can and should diversify in all sorts of ways:

- By asset type—shares, property and deposits
- By having investments onshore and offshore
- By having your investments spread around several industries
- By having different managers—some directly managed by you, but using a spread of different fund managers.

Diversification is just so important at this time of life—never forget that you are dealing with your life savings, that one major calamity in an undiversified portfolio could mean you have no good summers. When clients have large amounts of cash, perhaps because they have sold their business or a property, I suggest that they don't have all their cash with just one bank—banks go broke. I certainly would never like to see all of a client's managed funds with one fund manager, and am also uncomfortable when a client has all his or her wealth in investment property. There are plenty of examples of people who have stopped work to live well who have lost everything, sometimes through a company going broke, sometimes through fraud. The way to stop this happening to you is to arrange things to ensure that you could stand to lose any one investment without damaging your lifestyle too much.

Diversification will mean that your returns are lower. However, this is a time of life where investment returns are less important than the ultimate return of your capital. Having to manage and keep records for many different investments may also be something of a time-consuming bore, but that is the price for safety. Better for it to be a bit of a bore than to take an unsustainable loss.

A lot of people find the investment world very confusing—there seem to be so many investment types and options available. Anyone can be forgiven for feeling confused and wary of all the claims and counter-claims from the many different institutions promoting their own investment products. But when you really boil things down, there are only three types of investment you can make:

- Shares
- Property
- Interest-bearing deposits.

Everything else is either speculation, such as gold, art, antiques and commodities, or a means through which you can invest, such as unit trusts, syndicates and managed funds of all types. This last group is a vehicle in which you can invest. They work by investors pooling their money, appointing a manager and letting that manager invest in one of the three investment types or, indeed, in all of the investment types.

Of the three investment types, also called asset classes, shares and property are *ownership* investments because you own the investment. Interest-bearing deposits are a *debt* investment. Ownership and debt investments have different characteristics, as discussed in Chapter 16.

Before building a portfolio of Security Assets, there are three questions you must answer:

- How much of the portfolio will you manage yourself?
- How much will you put offshore?
- How much will you have in ownership investments?

How much of the portfolio will you manage yourself?

Your choice here is between investing via managed funds, such as unit trusts, investment trusts and syndicates, and investing directly yourself into shares, property and interest-earning deposits. For example, you could invest via a real estate investment trust or you could purchase a rental property or two, and you could invest via a share unit trust or select and purchase individual shares to build up a portfolio. The choice is between paying someone else to make investment choices for you or doing it yourself.

When you have started to ease back, you will have more time than you used to have—you might get a lot of satisfaction from using that time to actively manage your investments, even if you have never invested directly before. You will probably have the time to learn and gradually start to make more and more investment decisions yourself.

However, the good thing about managed funds is that you have a professional managing your investments for you— someone who is qualified and skilled at analysing the markets and making investment choices. Moreover, by investing in managed funds you will tend to own better-quality investments. This is particularly noticeable in property investment. You may have enough money only to buy one fairly ordinary rental property, but a real estate investment trust has enough capital to buy a wide range of really good buildings. I would rather own a small sliver of a trust or company with top-quality buildings than 100 per cent of a building that was ordinary. Furthermore, I do not want the hassles of management—I have enough to do without looking after tenants. The downside of investing through managed funds is that they cost—and these costs do eat into your returns.

On the whole, I think that a lot of people who have started to live off investment income can do quite a lot of their own investment management. It is a great interest and you will feel more in control. You don't need to have all of your investments made directly. Indeed, you probably shouldn't. For example, you might have your offshore investment money in managed funds and, possibly, your property allocation. I think that I have most of the skills to invest well, but we still have quite a lot of our money in managed funds. Remember also that this is not a decision that you have to make and stick to forever. You may decide to invest mostly through managed funds while you learn about investment, increasing the amount that you invest directly as you gain skill and confidence.

How much will you put offshore?

You need a good part of your money offshore but, certainly, it should not all be onshore. This is not so much because you will get better returns offshore, although you might because there are a lot more opportunities there, but rather it is about managing risk. The best way to think about this is to imagine some national calamity—say, foot and mouth disease wrecking agriculture, or a virulent SARS-type illness devastating the population. That could wreck the economy for a decade or more, and it would be very comforting to have some money in Europe or the United States.

If you are planning to travel quite a bit, you should have offshore investments in a currency like the US dollar, pounds sterling and euros as a natural hedge against the costs of travel within these countries.

Generally, I think that people should have 40–60 per cent of their investment capital offshore.

Investor style

Your style as an investor is essentially about how much of the investment process you are going to do yourself and how much you are going to get others to do for you. There are three main tasks involved in investing in and managing a portfolio:

1. Asset allocation. Set this according to your investor type, as discussed on page 133, and monitor it, continually observing the success of your investment strategy. As values within your portfolio change the percentages that you own in each asset class will also change, which will require you to rebalance periodically. This is the most important part of investment—it is where most of your investment performance will come from. Although investment professionals can do this for you, of all the investment functions this is the one that I really like clients to take charge of.
2. The management and custody of investments. For many this is a chore and a bore as they receive dividend and interest payments, annual reports, file documents, do tax returns etc. There are many financial firms who will take custody of your investments. You can follow the performance online and receive a comprehensive report at the end of each tax year for your tax return.
3. Investment selection. This is the choice of individual investments within each asset class—which particular bonds you will buy, which shares, etc. The vast majority of investors will take advice on this although there are plenty

of people who research investments themselves and use direct, no-frills brokers to execute their orders.

You can pick and choose which parts of this you want to do and which parts you do not want to do. Mostly this will depend on what you enjoy doing, and what you are good at, know about and feel comfortable doing. There will be a cost for each part that you have someone else do for you, but that cost is unlikely to be as great as the cost of doing parts of it yourself if you do it badly.

How much will you have in ownership investments?

Over long periods, while ownership investments do give better returns than debt investments, they are also more volatile and carry more risk of complete failure. As noted previously, conventional wisdom says that on retirement you sell out of ownership investments and invest very conservatively in bank deposits and government bonds. I think that this is too conservative for an early easing out of the workplace. You will be a long time dependent on income from your capital and you need the growth that shares and property give. Note that this growth is both income growth and capital growth, neither of which you will receive from interest-bearing deposits. There may be a few very wealthy people who could happily live on the returns from bonds and bank deposits—but not many. Most of us need to keep up with inflation at least, so that the spending power of our investment income is not eroded over time.

This is not to say that there is no place for debt investments in your portfolio—there certainly is.

You need some debt investments:

- To give you the ability to cash up quickly in emergencies
- To tide you over if your other investments have lean or downright bad times
- To give steady, very predictable income
- To have some investments that will not move in the same direction as the others in your portfolio, which is called co-relation in investment terms.

It is likely that over time you will change your allocation towards interest-bearing deposits or debt investments. As you get older—into your seventies, eighties and nineties—and the amount of time you have to make your investments work for you decreases, you may gradually come out of ownership investments and have more in debt investments. Ownership investments are necessary for those who have a longer time-frame because they give better returns over a decade or so. You are unlikely to have the ability to withstand much volatility as you get older. This is particularly so if you need to live off capital to any extent. The last thing you want is to get yourself into a position where you really need to cash up some shares—chances are that will come just at the wrong time, when the markets are in a down phase.

In your fifties and sixties, your portfolio might look like this:

Shares	40%
Property	20%
Deposits/bonds	40%

By the time you get into your eighties, it might look like this:

Shares	20%
Property	10%
Deposits/bonds	70%

By the time you are into your nineties, you may be 100 per cent in deposits.

Figure 19.2: Changes in a typical investment portfolio over time

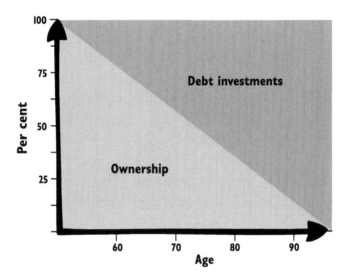

These are not meant to be model portfolios to be followed slavishly—building a portfolio is not about following someone else. We all have different positions in terms of:

- Our investment skill
- How much capital we have
- What returns we want and need

- When we will want the return of our capital
- The time we are prepared to put into managing our investments
- How much we worry about our money
- Whether we need to live off capital.

These factors are a mix that makes the building of an investment portfolio individual to you. Individualisation is the thing that makes managing money interesting—it is finding the right fit between the individual and their portfolio. Individualisation makes it very difficult to generalise in a book like this about the allocation you should make to each asset type. On the whole, however, I think that most people who have started to ease back should have quite a lot in growth assets—shares and property—and relatively little in debt investments. This is particularly true while you are still working to some extent. This allocation may change over time, as growth of both income and capital become less important and you can tolerate less risk.

The allocations when you start to ease back are probably in this range:

Shares	10–40%
Property	10–40%
Deposits/bonds	20–80%

If you still own a business or a part of a business, its value should be considered as part of the allocation to onshore shares. Note that no more than 80 per cent of your portfolio should be in a combination of shares and property—ownership investments—or, to put this around the other way, you should have at least 20 per cent in deposits—debt investments. I acknowledge that this is a very wide range, but that leaves plenty of room for individualisation to make allocations best suited to your investor type, as discussed on page 133. Furthermore, I cannot stress enough that these are the ranges for when you *start* to ease back. They will change as you get older.

Perhaps more important than anything else, take *time* and *advice* before you start to build your portfolio. If you are not sure—wait. If the markets seem overvalued—wait. There is nothing the matter with holding cash. Certainly over a long period you can do better than holding cash, but there are times when holding cash is a very useful position to take. Do not get panicked into what seems to be a very good market because that is what everyone else is doing. Do not be despondent and give up because you miss an especially good opportunity—rest assured, there will always be others. All your plans, and the wonderful life that you should have, can be dashed on the rocks of undue haste and greed.

20 | Managing investment risk: lakes and rivers

You must be ready for volatility and as such need to arrange your money so that you always have ready cash. Holding a good amount of cash at all times is critical if you are to be able to meet your expenses on an ongoing basis. Therefore you need to smooth out your investment returns by putting in a buffer. I see this as a lake of cash that acts as a reservoir. In good times, the returns from your investments will flow into the lake, raising the level. In bad times you are able to draw on the reservoir that you have created, thereby lowering the lake level. Having this lake that controls and buffers the flow of returns means that you do not have to sell your core investments during the bad times. For older investors, volatility can be a killer and it can wreck lives. If your money is not well arranged and you do not have enough cash, volatility can turn you into a forced seller of bonds, shares and property, just at the time when you should not be selling.

For a young person, volatility is not a great problem. People in their twenties, thirties, forties and some in their fifties can tolerate a lot of volatility because they have no need for their savings as their jobs give them their day-to-day income. They also have time to wait for the markets to rectify a major downturn with the major upturn that will eventually follow. These factors mean that younger people can afford to be very heavily weighted towards shares and property. The volatility shouldn't bother them and they know that they will get higher returns over time.

However, people who are dependent on their investments to give them income so that they can get on with enjoying a limited number of summers are in a completely different position. They cannot tolerate volatility. The ups and downs can wreck their lives, ruining every dream and plan that they had for their later years.

Markets are cyclical—good times follow bad times and vice versa. The worst thing that can happen is for you to become a forced seller—that is, to be in a position where you have to sell investments regardless of whether it is a good time or a bad time. Somehow, it is almost always bad times that people are forced to sell into. People can and do get caught in bad economic times when their returns are down and they have to sell out of some investment to use the capital to live on. They get poor prices for the investments that they sell and therefore have less capital when the market starts to rise again. Worse, many people will have nothing in certain markets because they have been forced to sell. They are out of the market and, so, do not enjoy the upturn when it eventually comes.

There is some simple mathematics that you need to be aware of: a relatively small fall in the markets needs a much bigger rise to put you back to the same position. If you had a 20 per cent fall in one of your investments, you would need a 25 per cent rise to be back to your starting point. For example, if you had $100,000 in shares and they fell by 20 per cent, you would have $80,000. To restore the value of your shares, you would need a 25 per cent rise in the market to get back to $100,000. You must avoid selling into downturns; you do not want to crystallise your losses. Nor do you want to sell into the bottom of a market slump because you will not then enjoy the bounce when it comes.

For young people, a year or two of poor or negative returns should not be of concern. Provided they do not get rattled out of the market by the negative noise, the markets will eventually come right. A young person should actually welcome volatility, as it creates opportunities. For older people, volatility will see your lifestyle affected—you will have to start to reuse those tea bags—and you should avoid it as much as possible while being prepared for what you cannot avoid. It is important, therefore, that you ignore a great deal of the investment advice in the media. This is largely aimed at younger investors and does not necessarily apply to you.

There is an old investment saying: 'Buy in gloom, sell in boom'. Most people do exactly the opposite. They buy when markets are booming and end up selling when markets are gloomy. They sell either because of the wall of negative noise that comes out of the markets or because they have to cash up to be able to pay the bills. Whichever it is, selling into gloom is a disaster and it is something that you must avoid, much like buying into boom means paying top price for your purchase, which is also best avoided. In that case it pays to wait.

You must have volatility

Although you do not want volatility, you need to have it. This is because volatility means that you will get higher returns. As I have said, the alternative to volatility is investing in areas that will give very low returns, such as bank deposits. Few of us have enough money to be able to accept such low returns so we have to increase our volatility risk. You should try to diversify out this volatility as far as you possibly can—but you will still have to be prepared for ups and downs.

Remember that investment risk is defined as the amount by which an investment deviates from the expected returns. These deviations can be on both the upside and the downside—sometimes an investment will provide returns that are superior and sometimes returns that are inferior. In fact, with most investments returns seldom fit neatly on the average, and if they do it is only for short periods of time.

Given that your portfolio is likely to always have either 'unders' or 'overs' from what is expected and that you need consistency to pay for the groceries, how do you manage your money and investments to always have the cash that you require to live?

A buffer

My answer to this is to put in a buffer—that is, the lake or reservoir discussed earlier—between your investment capital and your expenditure. This buffer takes the form of a bank account that is interest bearing but that is either on call or at least can be drawn on at fairly short notice. It should mostly be no more than ninety days. As such, this bank account represents a good part, and possibly even all, of the allocation that you make to cash deposits.

Ideally, this buffer account would hold an amount equivalent to at least a year of expenditure—preferably, it would hold an amount sufficient to live on for two years. Of course, not everyone will have this sort of cash but the thinking behind it is that the buffer account will mean that you do not have to sell investments to live on when times get tough. If you have two years' expenditure in an account, you can draw on that money when markets are down, which would be the worst time to sell assets. It is unlikely that your overall portfolio will show negative returns for more than two years, although it could if you are invested very aggressively. An amount of cash equivalent to two years of expenditure should give you a great deal of comfort and allow you to sit out the bad times. You will not, then, have to be a forced seller.

A lake and a river

The buffer account really works like putting a dam across a river and so providing storage of water in a lake. Imagine a river running unimpeded from its source in the mountains to the sea. When it rains the river rises, and if it rains a lot you get a deluge. When it does not rain and there is a drought, the river dries up. With an unimpeded river, rain goes straight into the river and the flow increases immediately. This is the same with your investments. When times are good you have a great deluge of returns coming into your account ready to spend, and when times are bad nothing comes in and you can't pay the bills.

If, however, you put a dam across the river, a lake will form. Water will run into this lake and the dam will control the amount of water coming out. Great deluges from heavy rain can be stored in the lake. The lake level will rise but the water can be held just the same. When there is a drought, you can continue to take water out as you draw on the lake's storage capacity. The level of the lake will lower but you will still have water to draw on because, unless there's a terrible drought, the lake will always have water in it.

Having a buffer bank account acts like a water-storage lake, allowing you a constant amount on which to live. Without the financial equivalent of a lake, you are dependent on regular rainfall. You have no reservoir to draw on when returns dry up.

Most financial-planning literature says that you should hold cash reserves of an amount equivalent to three months' spending. However, this benchmark is for younger people, who are likely to be working. Those of us who are dependent upon investment capital should have more cash as a reserve—at least one year and, preferably, two years. The reason for this is that in a severe market downturn, you could have negative returns for a year or even longer. You want to be able to live off this reserve while you wait for investment returns to normalise. Provided that you have a reasonably well-diversified portfolio, your overall returns should not be negative for longer than that. If they are, the world has real economic problems! The last thing that you want is to be forced to sell into such a serious market downturn.

Note that this reserve fund is not simply something to be drawn on when times are bad. In fact, the cash that you have in this account acts as a buffer, smoothing out returns in good times and bad. We all know that investment returns never come consistently and smoothly—there are always ups and downs. It is important that during good times returns go into this buffer account and are not spent, meaning that your spending should remain constant regardless of what your returns are. In my experience, buoyant times are nearly as dangerous as hard times. Long periods of strong investment returns are great—we all enjoy them. However, they can lead to thoughts and feelings which themselves lead to trouble. For example:

> My investment returns are fantastic. This investment game is easy. I have had good returns now for several years. This will carry on forever. We have more money now than we thought we would have. Let's have another trip overseas. Our returns from shares have been great. Let's put more into the market . . .

Dealing with market booms is as important as dealing with busts. Booms are a time to salt away the additional returns that you are getting. When a boom lasts several years, it is a great danger to assume that the markets will always be like this. Such hubris leads to higher spending and a lack of reserves. Eventually, booming markets will revert to the norm—there will be a bust. You need plenty salted away to continue to live through the bust.

As you sit and read this, you know that the investment game is not easy, that strong markets do not continue forever, that you cannot spend more than you have budgeted for, and that you should not move beyond your asset allocation limits. Of course, you may know this at the moment, but every day people get caught up in the emotional whirl of the markets and do things that they know, at least in hindsight, that they should not have.

It is important that super returns or returns above what are expected are put away against the poor returns that will come when the markets revert to the norm. In fact, I usually suggest to clients that they structure their affairs so that all investment returns go into the buffer account and that the required amount comes out of the buffer each month to cover living expenses. This is the only way that I can think of to smooth out investment returns, to be sure that you will have enough to live on and to make sure that you neither fall to the hubris that comes from success, nor get panicked out of the market when times get tough. This, along with regularly rebalancing your portfolio, should ensure that you have the money available that you want and expect.

Having this buffer account means that not only will the returns from both good and bad times be smoothed out, but returns that are irregular will also be smoothed. Most investments pay regular interest or dividends, although the time period varies—some pay monthly, others quarterly and some may pay out every six months. A lot of people depending on their investment capital to pay for their living expenses find this difficult—most supermarkets are not very interested in providing groceries on the basis that the dividend cheque from Rio Tinto is coming in a couple of months. The reservoir that is your buffer account can also smooth this irregular cash flow.

Buffer account

Everyone should have a buffer account to act as a lake on the river that is the flow of your investment returns. All income should come in to the buffer account, and an amount that has been established by doing a budget should come out regularly by automatic payment into your day-to-day account.

There are several things you should take on board when establishing a buffer account:

- Make sure that it is interest bearing. Many banks now pay quite high interest on on-call accounts, especially if you keep to their minimum balance requirements and use internet banking.
- Have at least one year, and preferably two years', expenditure in your buffer account. If you have income from sources that are not your investment capital and that are secure long term, such as superannuation payments, this can be deducted from the amount that you need to have in the account.
- Make sure that all your investment returns go into the account and that only the budgeted amount comes out.
- Use the buffer account to live on. Try not to sell out of investments when the markets are down.

Having a lake into which the river of your investment returns flow is a very important part of money management for people investing for income. Although your lumpy and uneven investment returns go into the account, a nice smooth flow of money will come out. This should remove the temptation to overspend in good times and allow you to keep spending when the markets are not performing.

21 | The place of property

Property can be a great Security Asset provided it is not mortgaged. Borrowing to buy property—gearing or leveraging—is a very good way to build up wealth. However, when you have debt on a property, the lender, usually a bank, will want to see its interest continuing to be paid regardless of what is happening to the property. If you lose a tenant and, so, lose your income when a property is mortgage free you have some problems. When you lose a tenant and your primary income when you have a mortgage, you have real problems. The biggest of these problems is called a bank, and it is not likely to show very much sympathy. That is why property is only a Security Asset if it has no or very little debt.

You have to acknowledge that property investors do, from time to time, have vacant properties that are not providing income. Sometimes this may only be for a couple of weeks, however, there are times when property, regardless of the type, can sit vacant for months. A younger person who is interested in property is often able to pay the interest by working a bit harder or finding some other income. It is more difficult for an older person. If you were only to lose the income from rents for a few months, you could probably go back to full-time work for a while—but losing the income *and* having to pay interest to a bank is a completely different story! Therefore, property works as a Security Asset, and sometimes a very good one, but only if it has no debt.

If the difference between a property being a Wealth-Creating Asset and a Security Asset is whether or not it has debt, you can convert it from one to the other by repaying the mortgage. Indeed, there are people who adopt something like this as their long-term financial strategy. They buy two or three rental properties when they are in their thirties, with the plan of spending the next twenty years or so paying off the mortgages. In this way they end up in their fifties with some debt-free properties providing good income on which they can live. This is a good strategy for a lot of people—the gradual repayment of debt can convert a Wealth-Creating Asset into a Security Asset at just the time you need it. The only thing you have to watch with this is that you might end up undiversified—that is, having a few properties, but not a lot else. There is nothing invested offshore or in the prime money-making activities of business or owning shares. Having property only is not a good investment strategy at the start of your twenty good summers.

Property is a good Security Asset because it tends to provide quite high income. Better still, over a long period that income is likely to grow. Even a fairly ordinary property is likely to at least match inflation, meaning that you have an income that is inflation indexed for the rest of your life. In fact, most property gives growth that betters inflation, thus making up for the investments in your portfolio that do not show income growth, such as bonds. You will also have capital growth from your properties, which is good for people who want to pass assets on to their children as an inheritance.

There are three disadvantages to property:

- It is usually a big, expensive asset that will, for a lot of people, make up a big proportion of the total investment portfolio. If the property part of your portfolio is represented by just one or two properties, you are subject to risk from having just one or two tenants in just one or two locations. This could leave you exposed to an event that could cost you dearly.

- The amount of money that is involved in property can mean that you go into property that is of fairly ordinary quality. While you do not have to buy the very best property in the very best location, you do want to buy things that are fairly good. These are expensive, and I do see people trying to stretch their money by purchasing things they would not otherwise buy.

- They require management. Property takes time to manage, residential property in particular. It is tempting to say that once you have eased back, you will have a lot more time and, so, will be able to manage rental property. While this is true for a lot of people, it is not true for everyone. I know people who have eased back and even ceased work completely to find themselves very busy, and wondering how they ever managed to fit in a proper job.

All three of these disadvantages—quality, lack of diversification and ongoing management—can be resolved by investing in property via managed funds. These are funds, such as listed property trusts and unit trusts, that own large numbers of properties, often worth hundreds of millions of dollars. They are all based on commercial property—retail and industrial properties and office space. Some target one particular type and at others spread around a range of property types. It is possible, indeed it is quite easy, to buy into a widely diversified holding of quality property via managed funds, using the amount of money that you choose. The downside of investing in property via managed funds is that you have to pay the management costs of the trust that owns the property. This will eat into returns. However, the quality of the property and the professional management should make up for this. If it doesn't, get out and find a better-performing fund.

I think, all else being equal, that people who are easing back should go into property directly if they have sufficient capital to avoid borrowings. Nonetheless, do not have too much in property—certainly it should be less than 50 per cent of your portfolio. Other people should not ignore property, but go into it via managed funds.

Commercial versus residential

When most people think of rental property, they automatically think of residential property. I think this is a shame, because there are quite significant benefits from owning particular types of commercial property. On the whole, I am a great fan of industrial property. This is because:

- It is very low maintenance—they are usually very simple buildings with four concrete walls and an iron roof.
- It has low obsolescence—the kitchen and bathroom do not go out of fashion every ten years or so.

- It is low management—tenants are often bound for years by a long-term lease and are responsible for a lot of the upkeep.
- It is relatively high yielding—the income compared to the purchase price is high.
- It is relatively low cost, making it within the price range of some private investors—compared to office buildings and retail, anyway.

The reason industrial property is not very popular with a lot of private investors is that it is not as readily understandable as residential property and the lease arrangements seem to be quite complicated. Furthermore, while industrial property is not as expensive as office buildings, it is usually more expensive than residential property. Nevertheless, as a good, steady income-earner with low maintenance and a low management–hassle factor, it is hard to beat industrial property.

Residential property works quite well as a Security Asset in most cases. However, the property you might own while building up your wealth could be quite different from what you own when you have eased back and are looking for income. Quite often, high capital-growth property is not likely to also give high income. Typically, high capital-growth properties are found in the very best locations, such as central city, desirable suburbs, but these areas are expensive and, so, do not give good income yields. These kinds of properties are very suitable for building up wealth, but are not likely to give you enough income on which to live. Less attractive locations will give you better yields, and it is these that I would seek out. I am not saying you should buy a tumbledown old building out in the boondocks, but nor do you have to buy into the very best street in town. Look for property that shows a good yield, but is well enough located so that it is likely always to have some demand from tenants. This new stage of life requires you to invest for income—capital growth is secondary.

22 | The place of shares

When you first start to take life easier, shares should make up a major part of your investment portfolio—in the 20–50 per cent range. Shares have many of the same attributes as property—they give good income, capital growth and income growth. But, they have two things that property does not have:

- Greater volatility—shares do show a lot of ups and downs, but overall, and over a long period, they show very good returns. However, they can thrash around a lot in a scary sort of way while they give those returns.
- Greater liquidity—unlike property, at most times shares are easy and cheap to cash up.

The volatility may be bad for some people. Although shares have always recovered from a major fall in the past, it can take a very long time, and it is certainly no fun knowing that the value of your life savings is significantly less than you planned for and may remain that way for some years. The way to manage volatility is to diversify—across countries, across industries and across individual companies.

Nonetheless, you also have to acknowledge that there is a close relationship between the values of shares across countries, industries and individual companies—they will quite often all tend to move in the same direction. Diversification will help the overall volatility of your share holdings, but not altogether eliminate it. The volatility is, to some extent, the price that you have to pay for the good returns that shares give over time.

Rattled out

About the worst thing that can happen to you, as an investor, is that you sell out before your investment has time to give its expected returns. This happens with shares more than any other investment—people find the volatility of the shares that they own greater and more difficult to tolerate than they thought possible.

We know that over long periods of time shares give the best returns, but they show a great deal of volatility in getting those returns. They need at least ten years and preferably twenty years for an investor to get the full measure of returns that shares should give: the longer the investment, the more likely that shares will give returns close to their long-run historic average of 10–11 per cent.

The problem is that many people do not get to enjoy these returns because they get rattled out of the market during times of high volatility. Frightened by the swings in value and the wall of noise coming out of the media, they sell out. Everyone knows that we are meant to buy in gloom when prices are low and sell in boom when prices are high, but it takes a bit of nerve to do.

It is important that you get your asset allocation right, as discussed on pages 139–140, so that you own a proportion of shares and property to give you the returns and exposure to volatility that you will be comfortable with over time. If in doubt, err on the conservative side, as you are better to have consistently lower returns than have the volatility rattle you out of the market at the wrong time.

Disasters can happen when people buy into shares, disasters not so much concerned with the shares themselves, but with the volatility they show. The disaster happens when people buy into shares when there is a boom. They get caught up with all the hype and the tales from family and friends about the vast profits made, so they buy in. Their timing is usually at, or near to, the height. Then they hold on while the market inevitably falls, selling out a year or two after purchase, right at the bottom. This is human nature, and although it is easy to say that you should do the opposite of what everyone else is doing—buying when everyone else is selling, and selling when everyone else is buying—it is hard to actually do. You can use the volatility of shares to your advantage, but it takes patience and fortitude to swim against the tide.

Liquidity, on the other hand, is an attractive feature of shares for some people. The ability to cash up quickly and relatively cheaply means that you can move out of a market when you feel the need. This can, of course, prove to be a disadvantage, too, as a few people will often move in and out of the market at just the wrong times. Nevertheless, the ability to turn your share investments into cash is an advantage of shares, especially for people who want or need to live off capital to some extent.

Growth or dividend yield

On the whole, shares that have high-dividend yields show lower income and capital growth than shares that have high capital growth but tend to have very low-dividend yields. While there have been plenty of exceptions to this rule, it works most of the time. Usually, people who have started to ease back look for shares with high-dividend yields to provide income. High-dividend-yield shares are often found in the utility sector—power and phone companies, and so on. Usually these companies not only pay out a lot of cash as dividends, but they are also safer than most—people continue to buy electricity even when there is an economic downturn. Property companies and trusts also fit this category. Often there are quite good dividend opportunities with some other industrial companies, although these may be more affected by adverse economic events. People who are depending on their investments for income usually look for companies in the utility and property sectors, and perhaps choose a few other companies that have a history of paying good dividends regularly.

However, you should not ignore growth companies. This is for two reasons:

- As growth companies increase their profitability, their dividends also increase. You may put $10,000 into a company and only get $300 in dividends in the first year. But if the company is successful the dividends increase and, say,

four years later you are getting $1,000 in dividends and
the share price will also have grown.

- Shares are liquid, so it is quite easy to take out some of
your capital profits by selling a small percentage of your
holdings. For example, you buy $10,000 worth of shares in
a company which is paying out no or, at most, very small
dividends. The share price grows over a year so that you
now have a holding worth $12,000. You can sell $2,000
worth of shares, taking out the capital profit you have made.
You could repeat this for as long as you like, perhaps not
taking out all of your capital profits, to allow for inflation.

Growth companies tend to give better returns to shareholders.
Even though they are often more risky and volatile, you should
have some in your portfolio. Any halfway decent sharebroker
should be able to build a portfolio for you, made up mostly of
high-dividend-yield shares with a smaller proportion of growth
shares. Look around—some brokers show on their websites
typical high-yield portfolios for clients needing income without
too much volatility.

You can also enhance your income by doing some selective
trading. This again is easier said than done, but one area that is
often fruitful is 'stagging'. This is to buy into an initial public
offering, often referred to as an IPO; that is, before a new
company lists. The shares will often come on to the market at
a premium, giving you a cash profit if you sell on the day of
listing if you have been lucky enough to get some of the shares.
You should not allocate much of your capital to trading—it
is risky. For most people even 5 per cent would be too much.

If you don't want to manage your own share portfolio,
you can opt for managed funds. You need to be fairly careful

with managed funds, however, as the fees charged by some of them can be very high. In particular, you should watch for high exit fees—some unit trusts put in a disincentive to selling by charging a fee for exiting, which may be higher if you exit within a certain time-frame. Brokerage houses and financial advisers will also manage your share portfolio (in fact, they will manage all your investments). They will do the stock picking for you, hold the shares in trust for you, bank the dividend cheques for you, do your tax returns for you, etc. Obviously they charge for this service, but it does have an advantage in that the portfolio is tailored specifically to you and your situation.

In summary, most people should have a significant proportion of their Security Assets in shares. A spread of shares with a heavy weighting towards utility companies or well-established companies should give good income along with some growth. Although shares are volatile, and can sometimes seem very scary, they do provide very good long-term returns. If you have just begun or are planning to ease back, you will still have a long investment time-frame—probably a decade or two, or three. Dividends from shares in many markets at the time of writing are fairly low. Over time, however, a well-diversified share portfolio will give good income returns with some growth, along with the ability to withdraw capital when it is needed.

23 | **Living on capital**

In easing back, some people will have to live on capital. If you think back to Chapter 9—factor one: how much capital do you have?, living on capital is one of the eight factors you can adjust and manipulate to be sure that you will have the income that you need. Living on capital requires two things:

- You need to accept that the inheritance you leave will be smaller than otherwise—even though the cheque to the undertaker might not bounce, you will have less to leave behind.
- You need to plan to accommodate the mechanics and practicalities of your choice, such as living longer than expected.

The acceptance of the fact that there will be less of an inheritance for the people you leave behind is a matter of personal philosophy. Philosophy, however, must sometimes be overridden by necessity. I think nearly everyone wants to leave something behind for their family. A reasonable compromise for people who do need to spend capital is to keep the house unencumbered and to use the capital from savings and investments only. It has to be said, however, that there will still be people who cannot afford to live as they want but will still pass on the value of the house untouched.

The practicalities can also be awkward. Remember the chicken farmer, discussed on pages 62–64. If you start to live on capital by killing chickens you will receive fewer income eggs. This will not make much difference at the start as you spend only a little capital, but as time goes on and more capital is spent, income returns will become less and less. Think of this like a mortgage that you are paying off over, say, twenty years. At the start, most of your monthly payments will be interest with only a little principal repayment. Over time this changes so that the last payment is mostly capital with only a small interest component. The bank will receive regular monthly payments, each of which is exactly the same. However, it will account for each payment differently, knowing that the interest and principal components differ over time. It also knows that one day the payments will finish.

The main difficulty with living off capital is threefold:

- How long can you do it for?
- When will it finish?
- Will you have to book into the local doss house?

It is relatively easy to work this out. You can go on to a banking website and put the numbers into a mortgage calculator. In using a mortgage calculator you are looking at this from the bank's point of view, working out how much the payments will be and for how long, given a certain amount of capital and assuming a particular rate of return. You put in the investment rate of return you think you will get (where the interest rate is), the amount of capital you have (where the loan amount is) and the amount of time you want it to last for. This will give you the total amount that you can draw each month. If this is not enough, you may have to adjust one or both of the variables—expected rate of return and length of time—until you get a suitable set of numbers. Using a mortgage calculator in this way will give you a theoretical amount that you can draw from your savings each month.

However, it is *only* theoretical, because the returns you get over a long period are unlikely to be smooth—there will be up times and down times. You should therefore be conservative with the numbers you put in. The whole point of this exercise is to ensure that the money does not run out before you do, leaving you resident in the doss house. Doing the numbers on a calculator like this will give you an indication, but it will not be something you can just set and forget. You will need to continually monitor what you have, adjusting as returns change over time. Perhaps most important is the amount of time your capital has to last. For most of us this will be a guess but it is a guess that should be made fairly conservatively, so set the time you want your capital to last a few years longer than you had first thought.

Annuities

Annuities can give you certainty. The purchase of an annuity will give you a set amount of income that may be inflation adjusted, if that is what you want, for a set period of time. In this respect it is very much like the reverse of a mortgage. With a mortgage, you take a large lump sum from the lender and you drip-feed it back with regular payments. In reverse, with an annuity you give someone—usually an insurance company—a lump sum and they drip-feed it back to you with regular payments.

An annuity is simplicity itself—the company takes your lump sum and pays it back with the investment returns over an agreed period. A variation is to buy an annuity for life; that is, the company will pay you an agreed monthly payment until you die. If you put all your wealth into an annuity for life, the cheque to the undertaker would, indeed, bounce. The actuaries at the company work out how long you are likely to live—if you die early they win, but if you hang on for years you win. There was an interesting case some time ago in France, where annuities are written by lawyers. A woman in her sixties took out an annuity. The lawyer died in his eighties, but the woman lived to be 122! Of course, the actuaries make sure that the odds are stacked in the company's favour—provided they have enough people taking annuities, they will have things worked out so that they stay on the right side of the ledger.

One of the downsides of annuities of this sort is that the investment returns are not likely to be high. The company will invest the money you give it very conservatively, and so the monthly payments will be worked out at a relatively low rate of return. You could probably do better investing yourself, but an annuity does provide convenience and certainty.

There is another form of annuity that is popular in some European countries in particular. In this annuity you use the house instead of a lump sum. The company takes a mortgage over the house and makes a monthly payment to you until you die or sell the house. When the house is sold, the company takes back the money it has paid you, plus interest charged. These annuities or mortgages on a house, often called home-equity release or reverse-annuity mortgages, are becoming increasingly common around the world. They are a way of being able to eat your house while you live in it.

Shares

It is fairly easy to access capital from a share portfolio, simply selling some of your shares as and when you need cash. The problem with this in practice is that you don't know what your returns might be when you come to sell as shares are volatile. You can never be certain how much you can cash up and still ensure that your money does not run out before you do. If you are selling shares, you should try to get the timing right by thinking well ahead and picking a time when the market is strong rather than being forced to sell into weakness.

Investment property

You can use capital to live on even when all your assets are in directly owned investment properties. If your investment-property rentals need to be supplemented by taking out some capital there can be challenges, but there are some options:

- If you have more than one property it is fairly easy to sell one.
- If you have only one investment property, you could access capital by selling a share in it, perhaps to a family member. This would see you with part of your capital cashed up, and a proportion of the rent still coming in.
- If the second option does not work and no one is willing to buy a part of your property, you can access part of the

capital you have in the property by borrowing; that is, taking a mortgage on the property. This will cut your income by the cost of the borrowing and it will add to the risk, but you should be able to increase the mortgage as you need more capital.

- Sell your investment property and have your property exposure via managed funds or real-estate investment funds that can be cashed up as you need.

Living on capital is an uncomfortable idea for a lot of people. If you have built up a lot of capital, you might never need to do so. But, if you need to there is almost always a way. Just make sure that you calculate the approximate amount of capital you can spend, and try to hold to that.

24 | Make every summer count

So, hopefully you've come to the end of this book inspired and feeling that if there was ever a time to get on with things, that time is now!

We all, at some point, talk about the things we would love to do. We all say things like 'I would love to learn to paint' or 'I would love to spend more time with my grandchildren' or 'I would love to go to Egypt . . . to work for a charity . . .'

The trouble is, we usually follow this statement with the word 'but', and then the reason why we are not going to do what we say we want to do. The idea of thinking about the number of good summers ahead is so you will drop the 'but' and start getting on with doing the things you would really like to do. Remember, you can and should have the life that you want.

In generations past, our final decades were often characterised by skimping and making do, without the means—wealth and health—to be actively engaged in hobbies and sports. However, with the improved general health and life expectancy for this generation together with some sound financial planning, there's no reason any more why our final decades can't be some of our best. If you know what you want you can make it happen, providing you have the will and determination to force the changes. If you are not going to grasp the life that you want now, you may never do so.

It is your job to figure out how you want to spend your next years and how to rearrange and unlock the capital that you have. This may require some drastic action—perhaps giving up your job, selling the house, going to night school, getting out of your business. All change is difficult, and radical change even more so. But, it is quite possible that radical change is what is required.

You may encounter some obstacles along the way. For example, family and friends may show surprise, or even alarm, at the changes you are going to make and you will most likely experience money concerns, either real or imagined. Your spouse may not be keen on having you working from home or selling one of the cars to help the budget, and so on. It is therefore important to keep sight of these two things if you are to overcome your obstacles:

- Maintain focus on the life you want so you are constantly reminded that what you're doing is worth it. You may have to make some hard choices, and you will only be able to face these if you are convinced, beyond doubt, that what you are doing is right for you.
- Plan—and plan early. More than anything I know, planning reduces fear of the future and fear of failure. Even a few ideas with some numbers scratched out on a sheet of paper will help defeat the insecurities that you might have. A more comprehensive plan made with the help of a good professional will obliterate them altogether.

There is still time to do all the things you have always wanted if you act firmly and decisively—there is no time for wishing, waiting and hoping. You have to cut to the chase and start living the life you have always wanted.

If you are not going to have some good summers now, when are you going to have them? This is a serious question, because you are never going to be fitter or more capable than you are now, you are never going to be in a better position to enjoy your life than you are now and you will never enjoy your time as much as you will now. If your life is not what you want it to be, change it. That may mean doing something quite radical, something that may raise the eyebrows of your family and friends. But it is *your* life—the only one you are likely to have, at least in this world—so it is time to get on with doing what you want. If there was ever a time to do the things you have always wanted to do, this is it. It's time to make every summer count.

Printed in Great Britain
by Amazon

12722720R00109